A Prayer
for Every Need

Publications International, Ltd.

Table of Contents

Talking with God

It can often be difficult to keep God in our lives. As we worry from day to day about the stresses of life, it's hard to take a step back and include God and his plan in our thoughts. We run around trying to satisfy others and take care of ourselves, we worry about the past and get anxious about the future, but we often forget to contemplate the present by talking to God—who is there for us at all times. He helps us during our hardest times and during our best. He continually watches over us with grace and mercy. Talking with God means praying to him, thanking him, asking him for help, contemplating his power and glory, reflecting on his beauty, and remembering to turn to him at any moment. The more we ponder the power of God the more our actions become loving, humble, and patient like his teachings.

A Prayer for Every Need is a personal reader of divine prayers, hymns, poems, and revelatory adages that bring our thoughts closer to God and his plan. As we contemplate what it means to be forgiven, we also learn how to forgive others. As we learn to heal, we also learn how to help others heal. With our thoughts given to God, our actions follow suit and we become more attuned to the plan God has for us. *A Prayer for Every Need* contains ten chapters that will help you with all of your needs, with prayers that bring you into a conversation with God during every moment.

Each page of *A Prayer for Every Need* is filled with devotional writings and prayers that can be read quickly whenever you may need them, providing meaningful and contemplative meditations on faith. You can read each chapter one page at a time or flip to a random page everyday; either way the inspiration and guidance you will receive from this book will fortify your relationship with God. Pray to him in thanksgiving, ask for guidance, rejoice in happiness, or heal from your hardships. *A Prayer for Every Need* covers a range of topics that fulfill the needs of the faithful. God is present in every situation, from the good to the bad, and it is with prayer that we can ask for his intervention along our journey. We must turn to him if we desire guidance, and it is with prayer that our divine and holy thoughts are transformed into the actions of the follower. God is listening and waiting for us to talk to him.

For Fortifying Faith

O love the Lord, all ye his saints: for the Lord preserveth
the faithful, and plentifully rewardeth the proud doer.
—Psalm 31:23

For Fortifying Faith

Let us draw near with a true heart in full assurance of faith, having our hearts sprinkled from an evil conscience, and our bodies washed with pure water.

—Hebrews 10:22

If you pray truly, you will feel within yourself a great assurance, and the angels will be your companions.

For Fortifying Faith

- ◆ -

Wherefore, if God so clothe the grass of the field, which to day is, and to morrow is cast into the oven, shall he not much more clothe you, O ye of little faith?

—Matthew 6:30

Dear Lord,

I am finding it hard to keep my faith strong when everything I do fails to produce results. My job is filled with complications. I have family members who are causing drama and making each other miserable. My health is not up to par and I am just tired down to the bone. My faith is wavering, Lord, and I ask that you help fortify my patience, trust, and resilience. I ask that you give me what I need to face my problems and move beyond them, stronger and wiser and happier. Help me to once again operate from a place of pure faith and trust in your will and your ways. Help me to feel as though everything makes sense again, Lord. Amen.

For Fortifying Faith

As for man, his days are as grass: as a flower of the field, so he flourisheth.

—Psalm 103:15

*E*ven in our toughest moments, Lord, we yearn to grow into fullest flower. Give us a faith as resilient and determined as dandelions pushing up through cracks in the pavement.

For Fortifying Faith

Watch ye, stand fast in the faith, quit you like men, be strong.

—1 Corinthians 16:13

Lord, Give me hope,

Give me patience to cope

And a reason to keep on trying.

Take my trembling hand

Give me power to stand

And a faith that is strong and undying.

For Fortifying Faith

❖

God,

Not a day goes by, dear God, when your faith in me doesn't show up as some small miracle in my life. I am in awe of your belief in me, even when I don't believe in myself. Your loving grace gives me the courage to do anything, and your trust in me strengthens my resolve. I am so grateful you see me through the eyes of a loving Father, and you never let me down or abandon me in my times of need. Thank you, God, for the faith that can move mountains, and for helping me to realize that with you beside me, all those mountains are nothing more than large hills that can be easily climbed. I cherish your faith in me, God. Amen.

For Fortifying Faith

As for God, his way is perfect; the word of the Lord is tried: he is a buckler to all them that trust in him.

—2 Samuel 22:31

Beloved Lord,

There are many things I don't know. People ask me questions about you that I can't answer. When scientific discussions or philosophical debates start up, I don't know what to say. I hear folks trying to disprove your power or your love or even your existence, and I know there's something missing in their arguments, but I can't say what. Still, I am not ashamed, because I know you. I have put my trust in you, and no fancy argument is going to change that. I may not know everything about you, but you are a reality in my life. Thank you.

For Fortifying Faith

Trust in the Lord with all thine heart; and lean not unto thine own understanding. In all thy ways acknowledge him, and he shall direct thy paths.

—Proverbs 3:5–6

Grant, O Lord, that we may live in thy fear, die in thy favour, rest in thy peace, rise in thy power, reign in thy glory.

—William Laud

For Fortifying Faith

❖

Know therefore that the Lord thy God, he is God, the faithful
God, which keepeth covenant and mercy with them that love him
and keep his commandments to a thousand generations . . .

—Deuteronomy 7:9

Dear God,

I pray today to have more faith in my own abilities. I
sometimes sell myself short and don't go out on a limb,
afraid to fail at something even if I really want to try it. I let
doubt scare me away and talk myself out of things, sure I
don't have what it takes to make them happen. Then I regret
never having gone after my dreams or feeling accomplished.
I know that you have faith in me, but how do I find that
faith for myself? Help me to recognize my own worth and
strength, and to see that I am far more capable than I
imagine myself to be. Help me to reach above and beyond
where I am to get to where I want to be and to feel happy
and fulfilled again. Amen.

For Fortifying Faith

Heavenly Father, what do I have to fear when you are the one caring for me? And yet, I do fear. Irrationally I fear, despite your faithfulness, despite your assurances, and despite your promises. Why do I still fear? I don't always understand my trembling heart and the shadows of things far smaller than you before which it cowers. Please liberate me from these lapses of trust. Free me to stand fearlessly, supported by faith and hope, in the center of your great love.

For Fortifying Faith

*The Lord hath heard my supplication;
the Lord will receive my prayer.*

—Psalm 6:9

Prayer is a powerful thing, for God has bound and tied himself thereto. None can believe how powerful prayer is, and what it is able to effect, but those who have learned it by experience.

—Martin Luther

For Fortifying Faith

Hast thou faith? have it to thyself before God. Happy is he that condemneth not himself in that thing which he alloweth.

—Romans 14:22

Dear Lord,

It's hard to face the day with hope, love, and faith when all I see on the morning news are stories of death and violence. Even if I don't watch, I hear about it from friends, see it on social networks and at my workplace. I pray for a powerful faith to hold onto as I try to understand why there is so much pain and suffering in the world. I pray for a steadfast awareness of your presence, and that there is a bigger picture behind the smaller pieces of life I see. Only you, Lord, know what that bigger picture is. I pray for the trust and the faith to live my life in love and light, despite any darkness around me. Amen.

For Fortifying Faith

The Christian on his knees sees more than
the philosopher on tiptoe.

—Dwight L. Moody

For Fortifying Faith

◆

Thank you, heavenly Father, for your promises. I trust that you will honor them in due time. Oh, it's no fun waiting. But I believe that you know what timing is best, and you have all the time in the world, and then some. Thank you, Lord, for the peaceful spirit you provide. Yes, I sometimes envy the arrogant, but I see the hole in their hearts. Thank you for the abundant life you provide me through faith.

For Fortifying Faith

*But the Lord is faithful, who shall stablish you,
and keep you from evil.*

—2 Thessalonians 3:3

Faith makes all evil good to us, and all good better; unbelief makes all good evil, and all evil worse. Faith laughs at the shaking of the spear; unbelief trembles at the shaking of a leaf, unbelief starves the soul; faith finds food in famine, and a table in the wilderness. In the greatest danger, faith said, "I have a great God." When outward strength is broken, faith rests on the promises. In the midst of sorrow, faith draws the string out of every trouble, and takes out the bitterness from every affliction.

—Robert Cecil

For Fortifying Faith

* ◆ *

*L*ord, if there is one thing I can use more of, it's faith. Good, strong, solid faith. Faith in the harmony and order of a world I can't comprehend. Faith in the goodness of a society I often distrust. Faith that my family will be protected and loved, even when I'm not there to protect and love them. Give me faith, Lord. Good, strong, solid faith.

For Fortifying Faith

Let us hold fast the profession of our faith without wavering;
(for he is faithful that promised;) . . .

—Hebrews 10:23

Dear God,

Thank you for giving me a powerful foundation of faith in my life. From this foundation, I am able to build so much peace, harmony, and happiness just by trusting in you and in your unceasing guidance. I walk in gratitude daily for the miraculous way having faith in your will seems to work. No matter what is going on around me, if I stand in faith, I stand strong. I pray that I always have this trust in your will to depend on, especially when my own will leads me astray. I pray that my life be a testament to others of the wonders that happen when we put our faith in you, God, where it belongs. Amen.

For Fortifying Faith

*For whatsoever is born of God overcometh the world: and this is
the victory that overcometh the world, even our faith.*

—1 John 5:4

Dear Lord,

Hear my prayer. I thank you for never losing faith in me,
and for never giving up on me. My problem is the ways of
the world cause me to lose faith in my fellow men and
woman, and in myself. I pray for a stronger faith in all of
your beloved children, even those that don't behave in ways
I approve of. I pray for the kind of trust in life that sees
beyond surface appearances and judgments. I pray today,
dear Lord, for a deeper bond with you so that no matter
what goes on in the world, I am at peace. Amen.

For Fortifying Faith

I will praise thee, O Lord, with my whole heart; I will shew forth all thy marvellous works.

—Psalm 9:1

What can I give Him,
Poor as I am?
If I were a shepherd,
I would give Him a lamb,
If I were a Wise Man
I would do my part,
Yet what can I give Him,
Give my heart.

—Christina Georgina Rossetti

For Fortifying Faith

Blessed be God, even the Father of our Lord Jesus Christ, the Father of mercies, and the God of all comfort . . .

—2 Corinthians 1:3

When you come to the end of your rope, and patience seems to fly away, settle back into God's waiting arms.

For Fortifying Faith

Now we have received, not the spirit of the world, but the spirit which is of God; that we might know the things that are freely given to us of God.

—1 Corinthians 2:12

*B*lessed and praised be the Lord, from whom comes all the good that we speak and think and do.

—Teresa of Avila

For Fortifying Faith

◆

God, teach me to not fear adversity. Help me to accept and face challenges; help me to overcome unkindness. God, let me remember that adversity breeds character— that we cannot necessarily control our responses to it. Grant me strength to respond to adversity with grace, and please guide me as I learn the tools to overcome life's ups and downs with faith in you and courage.

For Fortifying Faith

*O Lord, how manifold are thy works! in wisdom hast thou made
them all: the earth is full of thy riches.*

—Psalm 104:24

Be thou my vision, O Lord of my heart;
Naught be all else to me, save that thou art:
Thou my best thought, by day and by night,
Walking or sleeping, thy presence my light.
Riches I heed not, or man's empty praise,
Thou mine inheritance, now and always:
Thou and thou only, first in my heart,
High King of heaven, my treasure thou art.

—"Be Thou My Vision"

For Fortifying Faith

I face each day with certainty
And sleep without a fear,
For I know the Lord of Heaven
Has an angel standing near.

For Fortifying Faith

·◆·

Surely goodness and mercy shall follow me all the days of my life: and I will dwell in the house of the Lord forever.

—Psalm 23:6

I wonder who can really have faith in good anymore with so much bad in the world. Seeing the death and destruction makes me question my own faith, God. I am sorry to admit that. This is when I most need to turn to you in prayer, God, and to ask not just for help coping, but help in recovering my faith. I know your ways are mysterious and I cannot understand them, but please help me turn back to faith when fear threatens to overtake me. There is much love and good out there, God. Keep my eyes on the sun, and when darkness comes, keep my heart focused on your light to guide me through the night.

For Fortifying Faith

*The Lord looked down from heaven upon the children of men,
to see if there were any that did understand, and seek God.*

—Psalm 14:2

My faith looks up to thee
Thou Lamb of Calvary,
Savior Divine
Now hear me while I pray;
Take all my guilt away
O let me from this day
Be wholly Thine.

—Ray Palmer

For Fortifying Faith

The plants breathe out and we breathe in, not noticing the exchange. And so we walk with the angels, seldom noticing the company we keep.

For Fortifying Faith

***

Lord, give me the faith to take the next step, even when I don't know what lies ahead. Give me the assurance that even if I stumble and fall, you'll pick me up and put me back on the path. And give me the confidence that, even if I lose faith, you will never lose me.

For Fortifying Faith

But the scripture hath concluded all under sin,
that the promise by faith of Jesus Christ might be
given to them that believe.

—Galatians 3:22

Lord,

My faith in you fortifies me, and gives me strength. My
faith in you is like nourishment when I am hungry or
water when I am thirsty. It gives me life and energy and
hope. My faith in you overcomes all fears, doubts and
insecurities, knowing that it isn't me doing the work, but
you working through me. My faith in you is life-sustaining
and creates miracles big and small everywhere I go. The
results of my faith in you, Lord, are the abundant
blessings you shower upon me for simply believing and
trusting in you. Amen.

For Fortifying Faith

◆

*F*aith is a living, daring confidence in God's grace. It is so sure and certain that a man could stake his life on it a thousand times.

—Martin Luther

For Fortifying Faith

●━◆━●

God writes the gospel not in the Bible alone,
but on trees, and flowers, and clouds and stars.

—Martin Luther

For Fortifying Faith

— ◆ —

Human faith lives between two extremes, Lord: It's neither completely blind nor able to see everything. It has plenty of evidence when it steps out and trusts you, but it takes each step with a good many questions still unanswered. It's quite an adventure, this life of faith. Lord, I must confess that experiencing your faithfulness over time makes it easier to trust you with the unknown in life. Thank you for your unshakable devotion.

For Fortifying Faith

It is of the Lord's mercies that we are not consumed, because his compassions fail not. They are new every morning: great is thy faithfulness. The Lord is my portion, saith my soul; therefore will I hope in him.

—Lamentations 3:22–24

Dear God,

I pray today for your mercy and compassion. I'm struggling with life, wrestling against it and not allowing you to work your miracles through me. I pray for a release from the blocks that keep me from your love and guidance. I pray for a stronger, deeper faith in the perfection of my life, even if I can't make sense of it right now. I pray for more spiritual endurance and fortitude when I feel like giving up. I pray, God, for your constant and loving presence. Amen.

For Fortifying Faith

◆

*I*t is a faithful saying: For if we be dead with him, we
shall also live with him . . .

—2 Timothy 2:11

Faith is not merely praying
Upon our knees at night;
Faith is not merely straying
Through darkness into light;
Faith is not merely waiting
For glory that may be.
Faith is the brave endeavor,
The splendid enterprise,
The strength to serve, whatever
Conditions may arise.

—Anonymous

For Fortifying Faith

For where your treasure is, there will your heart be also.

—Matthew 6:21

I will tell you, I have heard . . . God has two dwellings, one in heaven and the other in the meek and thankful heart.

—Izaak Walton

For Fortifying Faith

—◆—

$\mathcal{L}$ord, I know you will show your goodness and faithfulness to me if I diligently seek you. The problem isn't your willingness to give, but my tendency to try to do everything by myself rather than leaning on and trusting in you. The silly inclination brings me needless stress and wastes precious time. Today, I endeavor to lay my needs and troubles at your feet the minute I begin to feel the least bit overwhelmed.

For Fortifying Faith

◆

May I have a moment to speak with you, O God? I know there is much going on in the world that requires your attention. It's just that sometimes I feel tension getting a grip on me and worry clouds my view. This distances me from you and from everything in my life. I pray for the freedom to worry less. I want to simply trust you more.

For Fortifying Faith

$\blacklozenge$

But my God shall supply all your need according to his riches in glory by Christ Jesus.

—Philippians 4:19

God of your goodness give me yourself, for you are sufficient for me. I cannot properly ask anything less, to be worthy of you. If I were to ask less, I should always be in want. In you alone do I have all.

—Julian of Norwich

For Fortifying Faith

The night is far spent, the day is at hand: let us therefore cast off the works of darkness, and let us put on the armour of light.

—Romans 13:12

Though like the wanderer,
The sun gone down,
Darkness be over me,
My rest a stone;
Yet in my dreams I'd be
Nearer, my God, to Thee,
Nearer to Thee!

. . .

Then, with my waking thoughts
Bright with Thy praise,
Out of my stony griefs,
Bethel I'll raise;
So by my woes to be
Nearer, my God, to Thee,
Nearer to Thee!

—Sarah Flower Adams

For Fortifying Faith

He who trusts himself is lost. He who trusts in God can do all things.

—Alphonsus Liguori

For Strength and Courage

Be strong and of a good courage, fear not, nor be afraid of them: for the Lord thy God, he it is that doth go with thee; he will not fail thee, nor forsake thee.

—Deuteronomy 31:6

For Strength and Courage

For thou art my lamp, O Lord:
and the Lord will lighten my darkness.

—2 Samuel 22:29

*L*ighten our darkness, Lord, we pray; and in your mercy defend us from all perils and dangers of this night; for the love of your only Son, our Savior Jesus Christ. Amen.

—Gelasian Sacramentary, "An Evening Prayer"

For Strength and Courage

Dear Lord,

I ask in prayer today for courage and strength to face some big challenges before me. I admit I am anxious, and even afraid, but I know in my heart you will never give me anything I cannot handle, and that you will be by my side the whole way. Instill in me a strong heart and spirit as I deal with my problems and keep my mind centered and focused on the solutions you set before me. I ask nothing more than your presence alongside me as I overcome these obstacles and learn the lessons each one has for my life. I thank you, Lord, for always being there for me in my times of need and struggle. Amen.

For Strength and Courage

◆

*L*ord, thank you for paying attention. Often I feel invisible, as if my wounds are hidden from everyone. I long for someone to understand me, to recognize my situation, to see that I need a helping hand or a kind word. But I can rest in the knowledge that you see me. You know exactly what I'm up against and precisely what I need. You listen to my cries for help and hear every syllable of my prayers. And that's why I pray to you now. Lord, please take a good look at my circumstances and step in to help me. Encourage me, enliven me, empower me.

For Strength and Courage

Strengthen ye the weak hands, and confirm the feeble knees.

—Isaiah 35:3

Lord, either lighten my burden or strengthen my back.

—Thomas Fuller

For Strength and Courage

Be of good courage, and let us play the men for our people,
and for the cities of our God: and the Lord do that
which seemeth him good.

—2 Samuel 10:12

God,

There are times when I act small in the world because I'm afraid to get out of my comfort zone. I'm scared of looking foolish, or failing terribly and letting people down. Yet, you've given me talents and abilities, and I long to use them for good in the world. Help me, God, to find that courageous lion within me and to go forward with trust and inner strength, knowing that whatever comes up, you'll help me through it. I pray for your will to be done in my life, and for the fearlessness that comes from having you as my rock and my foundation. Let me shine my light, God, and help me to not play it safe and miss out on the incredible experiences you have in store for me. Amen.

For Strength and Courage

O Lord never suffer us to think that we can stand by
ourselves, and not need thee.

—John Donne

For Strength and Courage

With him is strength and wisdom:
the deceived and the deceiver are his.

—Job 12:16

God is bigger than any problem you have. Whoever is opposing you is a weakling compared to God. Why not tap into God's supply of strength? Why focus on your problem when God is so much more interesting?

For Strength and Courage

The fear of man bringeth a snare:
but whoso putteth his trust in the Lord shall be safe.

—Proverbs 29:25

Dear Lord,

Thank you for the courage you've given me to pursue my dreams. So many of my friends have settled for lives filled with regrets and unfulfilled dreams, and I've been so blessed by you with the inner fire and drive to take my divinely-given talents and do something with them. No matter how hard I worked, I knew that I could not achieve such goals without you and I've always strived to keep your presence close at hand in all my decisions and choices. Thank you, Lord, for helping me find that extra strength within to face my fears, my doubts and my insecurities and go for a life well-lived. Amen.

For Strength and Courage

For the gifts and calling of God are without repentance.

—Romans 11:29

*L*ord, perfect for me what is lacking of thy gifts; of faith, help thou mine unbelief; of hope, establish my trembling hope; of love, kindle its smoking flax.

—Lancelot Andrewes

For Strength and Courage

*But they that wait upon the Lord shall renew their strength;
they shall mount up with wings as eagles; they shall run,
and not be weary; and they shall walk, and not faint.*

—Isaiah 40:31

Lord,

Make me strong in body and in spirit. Give me a faith that never weakens, and a courage that never wavers. Help me, Lord, to be a rock to those who need me, as you always are to me. Help me to also help myself when no one is around, and to learn to lean on your wisdom and guidance rather than my own. Be my rock and my shield, guarding me from harm. Amen.

For Strength and Courage

For when we were yet without strength,
in due time Christ died for the ungodly.

—Romans 5:6

$\mathcal{L}$et all the study of our heart be . . . to have our meditation wholly fixed in the life and in the holy teachings of Jesus Christ: for his teachings are of more virtue and of more . . . strength than are the teachings of all Angels and Saints.

—Thomas à Kempis

For Strength and Courage

Fear none of those things which thou shalt suffer: behold, the devil shall cast some of you into prison, that ye may be tried; and ye shall have tribulation ten days: be thou faithful unto death, and I will give thee a crown of life.

—Revelation 2:10

Dear Lord,

I pray for a strong spirit to stand against my fears today. I don't ask for fearlessness, because I do feel fear and I do worry and doubt. I am human. Instead, I pray that you will be at my side in frightening situations, and that you will never leave me abandoned and forgotten. I pray you will shore up my own spirit and give me a sharp mind and deep faith, so that I can overcome any blocks in the road to love, peace, and happiness. Lord, stand beside me and hold my hand, but also give me that extra bit of courage for the times you ask that I walk through the darkness alone. Thank you, Lord. Amen.

For Strength and Courage

The things, good Lord, that we pray for give us the grace to labour for.

—St. Thomas More

For Strength and Courage

Keep me as the apple of the eye,
hide me under the shadow of thy wings . . .

—Psalm 17:8

As storm clouds gathered, Father, I used to run for cover, panicked and picking a favorite escape. None of them worked for long, Dear God, and none of them kept me safe. No more running then. I see it clearly now: Wherever I am standing is a special place, under the shadow of your sheltering wing.

For Strength and Courage

The labour of the righteous tendeth to life:
the fruit of the wicked to sin.

—Proverbs 10:16

Thou, O God, dost sell us all good things at the price of labour.

—Leonardo da Vinci

For Strength and Courage

For then shalt thou lift up thy face without spot; yea, thou shalt be stedfast, and shalt not fear . . .

—Job 11:15

No matter what my ears may hear
Or what my eyes may see,
There's nothing for me to fear, Lord;
You're always here with me.

For Strength and Courage

I can do all things through Christ which strengtheneth me.

—Philippians 4:13

God,

Give me the wisdom to know what is important in life, and the courage to pursue those things. My life is such a blur lately, with an overload of obligations, information, and distractions coming at me to the point where I end up feeling so tired and worn down. I'm not getting things done, and failing to take care of my own health. Help me slow down and focus, and not be afraid to say no. Give me strength to tackle the important duties, which then leaves room for more fun in my life. Show me, God, balance and harmony between what I need to do for others, and what I need to replenish myself. Amen.

For Strength and Courage

Be not deceived; God is not mocked: for whatsoever a man soweth, that shall he also reap.

—Galatians 6:7

Be brave, my soul—
Let go of lies.
Stop deceiving yourself.
Have courage
To embrace the truth
And all its consequences.

For Strength and Courage

Defend the poor and fatherless:
do justice to the afflicted and needy.

—Psalm 82:3

I now make my earnest prayer that God would be most graciously pleased to dispose us all to do justice, to love mercy, and to demean ourselves with that charity, humility, and pacific temper of mind which were the characteristics of the divine author of our blessed religion.

—George Washington

For Strength and Courage

*But hath in due times manifested his word through preaching,
which is committed unto me according to the commandment
of God our Saviour.*

—Titus 1:3

Instead of asking yourself whether you believe it or not, ask yourself whether you have this day done one thing because he said, Do it, or once abstained because he said, Do not do it! It is simply absurd to say you believe, or even want to believe, in him, if you do not do anything he tells you.

—George MacDonald

For Strength and Courage

Continue patiently, believingly, perseveringly to wait upon God.

—George Muller

Lord, help me understand that the challenges I am going through serve to strengthen and empower me. Teach me the wisdom to discern that my trials mold me into something far grander than even I could have imagined.

For Strength and Courage

Finally, my brethren, be strong in the Lord, and in the power of his might. Put on the whole armour of God, that ye may be able to stand against the wiles of the devil.

—Ephesians 6:10–11

Dear God,

Give me strength today to stand against temptation. Empower me with the faith that I can say no to things that don't add to my peace or happiness without guilt or regret. Give me, God, the courage to turn away from things that might bring fleeting pleasure, but may not be your will for me. I ask today in prayer for the strength to do what is right, what is just and what is fair, even if I am tempted to cheat, lie, or take more than my fair share. Amen.

For Strength and Courage

The raging storm may round us beat,
A shelter in the time of storm;
We'll never leave our safe retreat,
A shelter in the time of storm.
Oh, Jesus is a Rock in a weary land,
A weary land, a weary land;
Oh, Jesus is a rock in a weary land,
A shelter in the time of storm.

—Vernon J. Charlesworth

For Strength and Courage

Abide in me, and I in you. As the branch cannot bear fruit of itself, except it abide in the vine; no more can ye, except ye abide in me.

—John 15:4

Abide with me,
Fast falls the eventide;
The darkness deepens;
Lord, with me abide!
When other helpers fail
And comforts flee,
Help of the helpless,
O abide with me.
I need thy presence
Every passing hour;
What but thy grace
Can foil the tempter's power?
Who like thyself,
My guide and stay can be?
Through cloud and sunshine,
Lord, abide with me.

—Henry F. Lyte

For Strength and Courage

◆

Wherever I go, Lord, some kind of temptation always confronts me. It could be as common as driving down the road and being tempted to be angry at another driver. Or it could be as uncommon as seeing someone in distress and being tempted to ignore that person. No single temptation is difficult to resist. It's the constant onslaught of temptations that wears me down. And when I'm fatigued and haggard, I just feel that I can't help myself. Cleanse my heart and my mind. And give me the power to repel evil and conquer the temptations that daily besiege me. I pray in the precious name of Jesus. Amen.

For Strength and Courage

No coward soul is mine
No trembler in the world's storm-troubled sphere:
I see heaven's glories shine,
And faith shines equal, arming me from fear.

—Emily Bronte

For Strength and Courage

◆

So often I have to put on a brave face, Lord, a smile just to get through an encounter or situation, but you see my heart. What would I do without you? How would I get through if I didn't have you as my place of refuge, the one who supports me from within? I'm leaning entirely on you even though no one else may know how much I'm struggling.

For Strength and Courage

Dear God,

It's been difficult lately. One challenge after another, one obstacle after the next. But I know everything is for my greatest growth and to teach me valuable lessons, and for that I come to you today to give thanks and praise. I may get angry and frustrated when life gets derailed, but I know in my heart you are never giving me more than I can handle, and that there is a blessing on the other side of each lesson you provide me with. Those blessings are what keep me going, even on the most troubling of days. Thank you for caring about me enough to push me and motivate me to grow, to become a stronger, better person through my trials and tribulations. I truly am blessed. Amen.

For Strength and Courage

The way of the Lord is strength to the upright:
but destruction shall be to the workers of iniquity.

—Proverbs 10:29

How can I resist a temptation that I have succumbed to time after time? My Creator, you have made me in your image, and yet I behave more like a beast who is out of control. Still it's only human to be sinful—or so my worldly friends tell me. Something that feels so good can't be so wrong! Our desires are who we are. Right? Wrong! You have told me that I must live a morally righteous life—even though it goes against my tendency to please myself. I must stop myself from surrendering to these temptations, and instead I must surrender to your will. I must place my life in your hands. But I can't do this on my own. I need your strength to resist and your holiness to be pure. Please clothe me in your righteousness.

For Strength and Courage

I am weak, but thou art mighty;
hold me with thy powerful hand.

—William Williams

For Strength and Courage

◆

So often I have to put on a brave face, Lord, a smile just to get through an encounter or situation, but you see my heart. What would I do without you? How would I get through if I didn't have you as my place of refuge, the one who supports me from within? I'm leaning entirely on you even though no one else may know how much I'm struggling.

For Strength and Courage

And thou shalt be secure, because there is hope; yea, thou shalt dig about thee, and thou shalt take thy rest in safety.

—Job 11:18

God Almighty, please help me to put everything into perspective. I want to be realistic but also optimistic. Please send me hope and give me strength of mind to make things right again. Amen.

For Strength and Courage

And where is now my hope? as for my hope, who shall see it?

—Job 17:15

I falter where I firmly trod,
And falling with my weight of cares
Upon the great world's altar stairs
That slope through darkness up to God,
I stretch lame hands of faith, and grope,
And gather dust and chaff, and call
To what I feel is Lord of all,
And faintly trust the larger hope.

—Alfred, Lord Tennyson

For Strength and Courage

⬤▬◆▬⬤

He will keep the feet of his saints, and the wicked shall be silent
in darkness; for by strength shall no man prevail.

—1 Samuel 2:9

I have been apart and I have lost my way . . . And in
my hours of darkness when I am not even sure there is
a thou hearing my call, I still call to thee with all my
heart. Hear the cry of my voice, clamoring from this
desert, for my soul is parched and my heart can barely
stand this longing.

—Gnostic Holy Eucharist

For Strength and Courage

O Lord, seek us, O Lord, find us
In Thy patient care;
Be Thy love before, behind us,
Round us, everywhere:
Lest the god of this world blind us,
Lest he speak us fair,
Lest he forge a chain to bind us,
Lest he bait a snare.
Turn not from us, call to mind us,
Find, embrace us, bear;
Be Thy Love before, behind us,
Round us everywhere.

—Christina Rossetti

For Strength and Courage

That they should seek the Lord, if haply they might feel after him, and find him, though he be not far from every one of us.

—Acts 17:27

I need thee ev'ry hour, Most gracious Lord;
No tender voice like thine Can peace afford.
I need thee ev'ry hour, Stay thou near by;
Temptations lose their pow'r When thou art nigh.
I need thee ev'ry hour, In joy or pain;
Come quickly and abide, Or life is vain.
I need thee ev'ry hour, Teach me thy will;
Thy promises so rich, In me fulfill.
I need thee ev'ry hour, Most Holy One
O make me thine indeed, Thou blessed Son.
I need thee, O I need thee;
Ev'ry hour I need!
O bless me now, My Savior, I come to thee.
Amen.

—Annie S. Hawks

For Strength and Courage

That he would grant you, according to the riches of his glory,
to be strengthened with might by his Spirit in the inner man.

—Ephesians 3:16

Sweet hour of prayer, sweet hour of prayer,
That calls me from a world of care
And bids me at my Father's throne
Make all my wants and wishes known!
In seasons of distress and grief,
My soul has often found relief,
And oft escaped the tempter's snare
By thy return, sweet hour of prayer.

—William Walford

For Strength and Courage

God is our refuge and strength, a very present help in trouble.

—Psalm 46:1

*H*eavenly Father, I want to be a faithful and obedient child, but there are times when I'm tempted to go my own way. I want to satisfy myself rather than serve you. I want to be free of your will to do what I please. My wants are terribly selfish, I know, Father. I have such a long way to go before I can be like the other men and women of faith I know and I've read about. You have so much patience to deal with me. I'm sorry, Father, for causing you so much trouble. Please forgive me and help me resist these urges to be selfish and to act independently of your will. I do want to please you.

For Strength and Courage

For thou hast been a strength to the poor, a strength to the needy in his distress, a refuge from the storm, a shadow from the heat, when the blast of the terrible ones is as a storm against the wall.

—Isaiah 25:4

God moves in a mysterious way
His wonders to perform
He plants his footsteps in the sea
And rides upon the storm.
Deep in unfathomable mines
Of never-failing skill
He treasures up his bright designs,
And works his sovereign will.
Ye fearful saints fresh courage take;
The clouds ye so much dread
Are big with mercy, and shall break
In blessings on your head.

—William Cowper, "Light Shining out of Darkness"

For Strength and Courage

Only be thou strong and very courageous, that thou mayest observe to do according to all the law, which Moses my servant commanded thee: turn not from it to the right hand or to the left, that thou mayest prosper withersoever thou goest.

—Joshua 1:7

Lord,

Guide my steps today so that I might help others and be a light in the world, especially for those who are weak and troubled. I pray for the courage to stand against injustices and to reach out to my fellow humans without fear or concern of the repercussions. I am ready to be a force for good, Lord. I am willing to step into a purpose that is founded in love and in spreading that love to all I meet. All I ask is that you direct my actions and keep me strong and pure in spirit. Amen.

For Strength and Courage

I arise today through the strength of heaven,
The light of the sun,
The radiance of the moon,
The splendor of fire,
The speed of lightning,
The swiftness of wind,
The depth of the sea,
The stability of the earth,
And the firmness of rock.

—St. Patrick, "St. Patrick's Breastplate"

For Strength and Courage

God grant me the serenity to accept the things
I cannot change, courage to change the things I can,
and wisdom to know the difference.

—Reinhold Niebuhr

For Strength and Courage

◆

For me, Lord God, the temptations of the mind are stronger than the temptations of the heart. When thoughts of sinning linger in my mind, I can't help but imagine how pleasurable it would be to succumb to a particular temptation. As I dwell upon it, I start to fantasize, creating a scenario of how that sin would take place moment by moment. And with each moment, my resistance weakens until I'm nearly lost. Cast these corrupting thoughts from my mind, Lord. Focus my attention on you. Help me to pray, for when my attention is on you, only righteous thoughts occupy my mind, and sin has no power over me.

For Strength and Courage

I laid me down and slept; I awaked; for the Lord sustained me.

—Psalm 3:5

*H*ave courage for the great sorrows of life and patience for the small ones; and when you have laboriously accomplished your daily task, go to sleep in peace. God is awake.

—Victor Hugo

For Strength and Courage

And there appeared an angel unto him from heaven,
strengthening him.

—Luke 22:43

God with me lying down,
God with me rising up,
God with me in each ray of light
Nor I a ray of joy without Him,
Nor one ray without Him.

Christ with me sleeping,
Christ with me waking,
Christ with me watching,
Every day and night,
Each day and night.
God with me protecting,
The Lord with me directing,
The Spirit with me strengthening,
For ever and for evermore,
Ever and evermore,
Amen.

—Celtic Prayer

For Hope

Blessed is the man that trusteth in the Lord, and whose hope the Lord is.
—Jeremiah 17:7

For Hope

Hope, like the glimmering taper's light,
Adorn and cheers our way;
And still, as darker grows the night,
Emits a brighter ray.

—Oliver Goldsmith

For Hope

But let us, who are of the day, be sober, putting on the breastplate of faith and love; and for an helmet, the hope of salvation.

—1 Thessalonians 5:8

God,

I am feeling tired and weary and weak. I do my best each day, and often it just doesn't seem good enough. I lose hope and enthusiasm and a sense of purpose to carry on. I pray today for restored hope in my heart, and a new vision of possibility in my soul. I pray you will assure me of better days to come, and that in the meantime, I am never alone in my struggles. I pray for a rejuvenated body with energy to continue to pursue my passions and dreams. Give me hope again, God, because my life is not over yet. Take my hand and pull me up just enough that I can get on my feet again and keep moving forward into the future. Amen.

For Hope

Who bids me hope, and in that charming word
Has peace and transport to my soul restor'd.

—George Lyttleton

For Hope

＊ ◆ ＊

From where I am standing, Father God, I have serious concerns about the future of our society. I'm seeing that the standard of right and wrong that used to unify us is quickly giving way to an anything-goes approach. I believe this puts us on shaky ground. What will become of future generations without the clear boundaries of your word and the clear direction of your truth? Help me, Lord! Encourage my heart with reminders that you are able to reach hearts that, though immersed in the cultural chaos of relativism, can by your spirit find a firm foundation in your good and eternal ways.

For Hope

The influence of his life, his words, and his death, have, from the first, been like leaven cast into the mass of humanity.

—Cunningham Geikie

I wait for the Lord, my soul doth wait,
and in his word do I hope.

—Psalm 130:5

O Lord, let me not live to be useless.

—John Wesley

For Hope

The Lord is good unto them that wait for him, to the soul that seeketh him. It is good that a man should both hope and quietly wait for the salvation of the Lord.

—Lamentations 3:25–26

Lord,

Give me hope for times when all seems hopeless. Give me strength for times when my own human weakness brings me down. Give me love when I feel alone and lost and misunderstood. I ask in prayer for a powerful sense of hope as I go forward to face my day. I know I'll face challenges, especially with other people. I know things won't always go my way. I know the news of the world will try to bring me to my knees. But hope, my Lord, will be the wings that keep me soaring when gravity tries to pull me back to the ways of the world, and the arms that hold me up when my own begin to fail me. Give me hope, Lord. Amen.

For Hope

*For we are saved by hope: but hope that is seen is not hope:
for what a man seeth, why doth he yet hope for?*

—Romans 8:24

The guardian angels of life sometimes fly so high
as to be beyond our sight, but they are always looking
down upon us.

—Jean Paul Richter

For Hope

◆

Worry and anxiety are exhausting, Lord Jesus. All those "what ifs" steal the pleasure of the blessings I have today. Please forgive me for the times I've given in to fear, allowing it to steal my joy. Help me focus on the wonderful promises you've made in your word. Teach me to reach for things of eternal worth, rather than for temporal things that come and go like the tide. Remind me that although life here on earth is full of the ebb and flow of change, I can put my trust in you—the one who is the same yesterday, today, forever.

For Hope

Abide thou with me, fear not: for he that seeketh my life seeketh thy life: but with me thou shalt be in safeguard.

—1 Samuel 22:23

Yet, in the maddening maze of things,
And tossed by storm and flood,
To one fixed trust my spirit clings;
I know that God is good!

. . .

I know not where His islands lift
Their fronded palms in air;
I only know I cannot drift
Beyond His love and care.

—John Greenleaf Whittier, "The Eternal Goodness"

For Hope

◆

One day at a time, Lord, right? However much I might wish to rush into the future or retreat into the past, it is only this day, this moment that you call me to live in. I cannot undo what's been done, and I cannot control what is yet to come. And while those things are out of my hands, you have given me the power to do three vital things right now: to forgive and see forgiveness for the past, to choose wisely right now, and to entrust the future to you. By your grace, Lord Jesus, I will do these things today, and I won't fret about the rest. Amen.

For Hope

One person who has mastered life is better than a thousand persons who have mastered only the contents of books, but no one can get anything out of life without God.

—Meister Eckhardt

For Hope

Be of good courage, and he shall strengthen your heart, all ye that hope in the Lord.

—Psalm 31:24

I'm so anxious to know what lies ahead. The suspense is almost more than I can take, Lord. Instead of trusting that you're going to work things out. I'm worried it might not turn out as I'd hoped. But if I did know the future, I'd probably lie awake worrying about that, wouldn't I? Ah, Sovereign Lord! What is my relationship worth if I don't have faith in your goodness and power and love for me? I lay these worries at your feet—once again. Forgive me for picking them up over and over. You are worthy of my full confidence.

For Hope

Thou art my hiding place and my shield: I hope in thy word.

—Psalm 119:116

When you have no helpers, see all your helpers in God. When you have many helpers, see God in all your helpers. When you have nothing but God, see all in God; when you have everything, see God in everything. Under all conditions, stay thy heart only on the Lord.

—Charles Haddon Spurgeon

For Hope

◆

My situation is uncertain, Father. The only control I have in the matter right now is how I choose to approach it. Will I stress and wring my hands and have the background noise of anxiety running through my head all day, even when I'm doing other things? Or will I take a deep breath, acknowledge the reality, and then choose to trust you to show me the way through it? That is the choice before me; that is the role I must play. Help me not to run ahead with presumptions but to wait and proceed as you clear a path for my feet. If you have actions for me to take or words for me to say, I trust you will make those clear to me. I'm choosing right now to trust you.

For Hope

And patience, experience; and experience, hope . . .

—Romans 5:4

God's plans, like lilies, pure and white, unfold;
We must not tear the close-shut leaves apart;
Time will reveal the chalices of gold.

—Mary Louise Riley Smith

For Hope

Dear Lord, when I look at a simple blade of grass and consider how many such blades you cause to grow all over the earth, I realize the miracle is so common I can easily miss it. Yet can I make one blade of grass—just once—come into existence from nothing, as you did when you made the heavens and the earth? I cannot. Remind me again, Lord, that you effortlessly sustain the whole universe and everything in it. You see it on the largest and smallest of scales, and you attend to every detail without straining your power one bit. Why do I worry, then, that you won't take care of what concerns me today? I will come to you, even now, and unburden my heart. Then I'll crawl like a young child into your everlasting arms and trust you to carry me. Thank you, Lord of my life.

For Hope

Ye ask, and receive not, because ye ask amiss, that ye may consume it upon your lusts.

—James 4:3

God answers sharp and sudden on some prayers.
And thrusts the thing we have prayed for in our face,
A gauntlet with a gift in't.

—Elizabeth Barrett Browning, "Aurora Leigh"

For Hope

*For we through the Spirit wait for the hope
of righteousness by faith.*

—Galatians 5:5

Dear Lord,

I am feeling more hopeful these days. For awhile, I forgot
to include your loving guidance and grace in my life. I
forgot that if I pray and meditate and just get silent
enough to listen, you always give me the answers I seek,
and the direction I need to overcome anything life hands
me. I pray for continued guidance and wisdom, and that I
may always live from a place of hope instead of fear, and a
place of possibilities instead of limitations. You are my
wings and my rock, allowing me to both soar higher and
stay grounded. No matter what I may be facing, staying in
the comforting light of your presence gives me the hope I
need to carry on with my head held high and my heart
strong and fearless. Thank you for the gift of hope. Amen.

For Hope

For if there be first a willing mind, it is accepted according to that a man hath, and not according to that he hath not.

—2 Corinthians 8:12

I am only one,
But still I am one.
I cannot do everything,
But still I can do something;
And because I cannot do everything
I will not refuse to do the something that
I can do.

—Edward Everett Hale

For Hope

Beareth all things, believeth all things, hopeth all things, endureth all things.

—1 Corinthians 13:7

The root of faith produces the flower of heart-joy. We may not at the first rejoice, but it comes in due time. We trust the Lord when we are sad, and in due season he so answers our confidence that our faith turns to fruition and we rejoice in the Lord. Doubt breeds distress, but trust means joy in the long run. . . .

Let us meditate upon the Lord's holy name, that we may trust him the better and rejoice the more readily. He is in character holy, just, true, gracious, faithful, and unchanging. Is not such a God to be trusted? He is allwise, almighty, and everywhere present; can we not cheerfully rely on Him? . . . They that know thy name will trust thee; and they that trust thee will rejoice in thee, O Lord.

—Charles Spurgeon

For Hope

Hope is faith holding out its hand in the dark.

—George Iles

For Hope

Wherefore gird up the loins of your mind, be sober, and hope to the end for the grace that is to be brought unto you at the revelation of Jesus Christ . . .

—1 Peter 1:13

Dear God,

I've lost so much in the last few years. Friends and family have passed away. Dreams have come and gone. Finances have been a problem and I find myself losing hope. I ask in prayer for a renewal in my spirit. I know you never bring experiences into my life without a purpose, but please help me to stay in hope as I get through them and learn the lessons they are meant to give me. When everyone around me seems too busy and I am alone, be my constant friend and companion. When circumstances keep occurring that test my strength and soul, flood my heart with hope and refresh my mind with new solutions. I don't ask for an easy life, God, just that when things aren't so easy, I never, ever lose hope. Amen.

For Hope

—◆—

Looking for that blessed hope, and the glorious appearing of the great God and our Saviour Jesus Christ . . .

—Titus 2:13

No darkness is black enough to hide you, Lord, for there is always light even if I sometimes misplace it. Just when I'm ready to give up, there it shines through caregivers, family, friends, through my renewed energy to choose treatments and recovery. I'm absolutely certain you are the sender of this light.

For Hope

*Now faith is the substance of things hoped for,
the evidence of things not seen.*

—Hebrews 11:1

*L*ord, you are the light I follow down this long, dark tunnel. You are the voice that whispers, urging me onward when this wall of sorrow seems insurmountable. You are the hand that reaches out and grabs mine when I feel as if I'm sinking in despair. You alone, Lord, are the waters that fill me when I am dried of all hope and faith. I thank you, Lord, for although I may feel like giving up, you have not given up on me. Amen.

For Hope

For there is hope of a tree, if it be cut down, that it will sprout again, and that the tender branch thereof will not cease.

—Job 14:7

One song can spark a moment,
One flower can wake the dream.
One tree can start a forest,
One bird can herald spring.
One smile begins a friendship,
One hand clasp lifts a soul.
One star can guide a ship at sea,
One word can frame the goal.
One vote can change a nation,
One sunbeam lights a room.
One candle wipes out darkness,
One laugh will conquer gloom.

—Author Unknown

For Hope

But if we hope for that we see not,
then do we with patience wait for it.

—Romans 8:25

If you would have God hear you when you pray,
you must hear Him when He speaks.

—Thomas Benton Brooks

For Hope

*Turn us again, O God, and cause thy face to shine;
and we shall be saved.*

—Psalm 80:3

As the great eye of heaven shined bright,
And made a sunshine in the shady place.

—Edmund Spenser

For Hope

O welcome pure-ey'd Faith, white-handed Hope,
Thou hovering angel girt with golden wings . . .
I see you visibly and now believe
That he, the Supreme good . . .
Would send a glistening Guardian if need were
To keep my life and honor unassailed.

—John Milton

For Hope

Preserve me, O God: for in thee do I put my trust.

—Psalm 16:1

$\mathcal{I}$ believe in some blending of hope and sunshine sweetening the worse lots. I believe that this life is not all; neither the beginning nor the end. I believe while I tremble; I trust while I weep.

—Charlotte Brontë

For Hope

That whosoever believeth in him should not perish,
but have eternal life.

—John 3:15

We live in deeds, not years; in thoughts, not breaths;
In feelings, not in figures on a dial.
We should count time by heart-throbs.
He who thinks most, feels the noblest, acts the best.
Life's but a mean unto an end; that end
Beginning, mean, and end to all things—God.

—Philip James Bailey

For Hope

Every word of God is pure: he is a shield unto them that put their trust in him.

—Proverbs 30:5

How sweet the name of Jesus sounds
In a believer's ear!
It soothes his sorrows, heals his wounds,
And drives away his fear.

—John Newton

For Hope

＊ ◆ ＊

To spend time praising you, Jesus, is like a strong antidote to whatever is burdening my heart. When I lift up my voice to praise you, in word or in song, the heaviness in my soul lifts too. I know your word says that you give "the garment of praise for the spirit of heaviness" to those who belong to you. I guess that's a more poetic way of saying it, but however it's said, it's true! Your word is true. Praise seems counterintuitive when things aren't going well, but when I trust your wisdom and just do it, it works every time.

For Hope

It is good that a man should both hope and quietly wait for the salvation of the Lord.

—Lamentations 3:26

Grow old along with me!
The best is yet to be,
The last of life, for which the first was made;
Our times are in his hand
Who saith, "A whole I planned,
Youth shows but half;
trust God:
See all, nor be afraid."

—Robert Browning

For Hope

$\mathcal{B}$egin to weave and God will give the thread.

—German proverb

To the only wise God our Saviour, be glory and majesty,
dominion and power, both now and ever. Amen.

—Jude 1:25

$\mathcal{W}$ithout Christ there is no hope.

—Charles Spurgeon

For Peace and Understanding

inally, brethren, farewell. Be perfect, be of good comfort, be of one mind, live in peace; and the God of love and peace shall be with you.

—1 Corinthians 13:11

For Peace and Understanding

Let us therefore follow after the things which make for peace, and things wherewith one may edify another.

—Romans 14:19

Lord,

I seek the wisdom of understanding, and the grace of peace. The world is becoming a hostile place and only those armed with your loving care seem able to find their way, and then light the way for others who are lost in the darkness. I ask from you a strong center from which I may go forth into the world and spread that same peace and that same understanding to others that need it so badly. Make me an instrument of your peace today, dear Lord. Let me help others find their center within where you reside, always loving, always caring, and forever present. Amen.

For Peace and Understanding

I am thy servant; give me understanding, that I may know thy testimonies.

—Psalm 119:125

Understanding is the reward of faith. So do not seek to understand in order to believe, but believe so that you may understand.

—St. Augustine

For Peace and Understanding

$\mathcal{P}$eace in daily work is the consciousness of health and ability to spare so that when one's tasks are done there is a margin all around. Peace in business is the consciousness of capital and plenty, so that one need not fear what the day may bring. Peace in the family is the consciousness that, under all the strains inevitably incident to the running of a home, there is an unfailing wealth of love and devotion and fidelity to fall back upon. Peace in the soul is the consciousness that, however difficult life may be, we are not living it alone . . .

—Harry Emerson Fosdick

For Peace and Understanding

Dear Lord,

The promise of your peace is what I long for right now. With all the chaos of my day-to-day life, nothing sounds sweeter than the quiet calm of knowing you are with me always, as a place of rest and calm I can turn to at any time. I ask for the peace only your constant and enduring presence can bring. Thank you, Lord, for returning me to balance and tranquility no matter how bad the storms are around me. Amen.

For Peace and Understanding

Who comforteth us in all our tribulation, that we may be able to comfort them which are in any trouble, by the comfort where with we ourselves are comforted of God.

—2 Corinthians 1:4

God does not comfort us to make us comfortable, but to make us comforters.

—John Henry Jowett

For Peace and Understanding

Heavenly Father, our diversions seem great. We can't remember when the insurmountable demands started piling up, and we have a hard time seeing the end. Allow us to take a moment from our hectic days to close our eyes and feel your peace. We ask you to lead us. Amen.

For Peace and Understanding

Dear God,

Everything in my life lately seems to be going wrong.
People are uncaring. Things I've worked hard for don't
seem to be coming to fruition. Everyone needs my time
and attention and I feel so tired and overwhelmed and
stressed. I ask today in prayer for peace, for serenity. I
don't ask for a removal of my problems, but for the power
and fortitude to deal with them as they arise from a place
of calm and stillness within. I know that you can provide
me that kind of amazing, unerring peace, God. Be the
rock upon which I can take comfort and rest when the
world spins out of control all around me. Be my peace
everlasting, dear God. Amen.

For Peace and Understanding

Depart from evil, and do good; seek peace, and pursue it.

—Psalm 34:14

Deep peace of the running waves to you.
Deep peace of the flowing air to you.
Deep peace of the smiling stars to you.
Deep peace of the quiet earth to you.
Deep peace of the watching shepherds to you.
Deep peace of the Son of Peace to you.

—Gaelic Prayer

For Peace and Understanding

Give me understanding, and I shall keep thy law; yea, I shall observe it with my whole heart.

—Psalm 119:34

Lord,

I know that I am only human, and not meant to understand your mysterious ways. To me, life sometimes makes no sense, and things happen that I just can't wrap my mind around. Please help me have a sense of peace, a sense of understanding that it all does make sense, and that everything happens for a reason, even if you are the only one who knows what that reason is. Help me feel more balance, harmony, and serenity even when I'm afraid and uncertain. Your love alone can make me feel as though everything is just the way it was meant to be, and that my life does have purpose and meaning. Thank you, Lord. Amen.

For Peace and Understanding

What I tell you in darkness, that speak ye in light: and what ye hear in the ear, that preach ye upon the housetops.

—Matthew 10:27

I am feeling my way in this darkness, God, and it seems I'm going in circles. Yet you have reminded me—quietly, just now—that encircled by your love with every move in any direction I go no closer to you—nor farther either—than already centered I am.

For Peace and Understanding

My mouth shall speak of wisdom; and the meditation of my heart shall be of understanding.

—Psalm 49:3

Lord, grant me a simple, kind, open, believing, loving and generous heart, worthy of being your dwelling place.

—John Sergieff

For Peace and Understanding

Great peace have they which love thy law:
and nothing shall offend them.

—Psalm 119:165

Your peace is like the sweet calm air after a storm, like a warm blanket on a cold winter day, like a happy smile of someone I love on a day when nothing has gone right. Your peace brings me the comfort and the strength I need to get through the hardest of times and the thickest of situations. I am so grateful, God, for the kind of peace your presence offers me, a peace so deep and abiding I know that no matter what is happening, that peace is there for me to tap into. Like an overflowing well at the center of my being, your presence is the water that quenches my thirst and gives me renewed vigor and life. Thank you, God, for your everlasting peace. Amen.

For Peace and Understanding

And the Lord said, Behold, the people is one, and they have all one language; and this they begin to do: and now nothing will be restrained from them, which they have imagined to do.

—Genesis 11:6

Whether we admit it or not, we all long to feel welcomed and accepted by others. Just as Jesus connected with people outside his circle of disciples, we need to connect with people outside our comfort zone and mirror God's acceptance of all people.

For Peace and Understanding

For the kingdom of God is not meat and drink; but righteousness, and peace, and joy in the Holy Ghost.

—Romans 14:17

Yes, Father in heaven, often have we found that the world cannot give us peace, O but make us feel that thou art able to give us peace; let us know the truth of thy promise: that the whole world may not be able to take away thy peace.

—Soren Kierkegaard

For Peace and Understanding

If any of you lack wisdom, let him ask of God, that giveth to all men liberally, and upbraideth not; and it shall be given him.

—James 1:5

Dear Lord,

I pray for wisdom and understanding for my fellow humans. So often my family, friends, and colleagues get on my nerves and create chaos and drama, and I find myself wanting to turn away from them. I know they are as human and flawed as I am, but my patience is short and my temper quick. Please help me to look beyond their behaviors to the sweet and wonderful souls they are inside, and to understand where their own fears and frustrations are coming from. Rarely is it even personal, so help me to also stop taking it all so personally and just be there for them on good days and on bad, as a true friend would, without judgment or anger. Amen.

For Peace and Understanding

*And he arose, and rebuked the wind, and said unto the sea,
Peace, be still. And the wind ceased, and there was a great calm.*

—Mark 4:39

Of all good gifts that the Lord lets fall,
Is not silence the best of all?
The deep, sweet hush when the song is closed,
And every sound but a voiceless ghost;
And every sigh, as we listening leant,
A breathless quiet of vast content?
The laughs we laughed have a purer ring
With but their memory echoing;
So of all good gifts that the Lord lets fall,
Is not silence the best of all?

—James Whitcomb Riley

For Peace and Understanding

God,

Give me peace of mind today, for I am worried about so many things. Give me peace of heart today, for I am fearful of challenges before me. Give me peace of spirit today, for I am in a state of confusion and chaos. I ask, God, for your peace today, and every day, to help keep my feet on the right path and my faith solid and unmoving. Without peace, I don't see the answers you place before me. Without peace, I cannot hear your still, small voice within. Shower me today with your loving peace, God, and all will be well in my mind, heart and spirit. Amen.

For Peace and Understanding

Speak, move, act in peace, as if you were in prayer.
In truth, this is prayer.

—Francois de Salignace de La Mothe Fenelon

For Peace and Understanding

These things I have spoken unto you, that in me ye might have peace. In the world ye shall have tribulation: but be of good cheer; I have overcome the world.

—John 16:33

Jesus loves the little children
All the children of the world.
Red and yellow, black and white
They are precious in His sight
Jesus loves the little children of the world.

—Rev. C.H. Woolston

For Peace and Understanding

Not that I speak in respect of want: for I have learned, in whatsoever state I am, therewith to be content.

—Philippians 4:11

When peace, like a river, attendeth my way.

When sorrows like sea billows roll;

Whatever my lot, thou hast taught me to say,

It is well, it is well with my soul.

It is well with my soul, it is well, it is well with my soul.

—Horatio G. Spafford

For Peace and Understanding

And whosoever will be chief among you,
let him be your servant.

—Matthew 20:27

$\mathcal{I}$f we are devoted to the cause of humanity, we shall soon be crushed and broken-hearted . . . but if our motive is love to God, no ingratitude can hinder us from serving our fellow men.

—Oswald Chambers

For Peace and Understanding

For other foundation can no man lay than that is laid, which is Jesus Christ.

— 1 Corinthians 3:11

Dear Lord, help me to build on a firm foundation by relying on your wisdom, diligently seeking your direction in all I do, learning to walk in your paths of kindness, peace, and justice to my fellowman. In Jesus' name, Amen.

For Peace and Understanding

A wise man will hear, and will increase learning; and a man of understanding shall attain unto wise counsels.

—Proverbs 1:5

The best listeners are often silent, the depth of their understanding revealed by their actions. God is one such listener.

For Peace and Understanding

In His will is our peace.

—Dante Alighieri

For Peace and Understanding

◆

I sing out in praise today, for the Lord has made me whole. My life is filled with peace and balance, and harmony is the order of my day. My life was not always like this. I once took on way more than I should have, and it wore me down. But in God's love, I now stand restored and at peace with whatever each new day brings. I know in my heart that I can handle anything as long as I am connected to the source that is my God. It is a source from which I can find all the highest and best blessings life has to offer. It is a source of pure peace.

For Peace and Understanding

I will praise thee; for I am fearfully and wonderfully made:
marvellous are thy works; and that my soul knoweth right well.

—Psalm 139:14

All things bright and beautiful,
All creatures great and small,
All things wise and wonderful,
The Lord God made them all.

—Cecil Frances Alexander

For Peace and Understanding

Or let him take hold of my strength, that he may make peace with me; and he shall make peace with me.

—Isaiah 27:5

Lord, make me an instrument of your peace;
where there is hatred, let me sow love;
where there is injury, pardon;
where there is doubt, faith;
where there is despair, hope;
where there is darkness, light;
and where there is sadness, joy.
Divine Master, grant that I may not so much seek to be
consoled as to console;
to be understood as to understand;
to be loved as to love.
For it is in giving that we receive,
it is in pardoning that we are pardoned,
and it is in dying that we are born to eternal life.

—St. Francis of Assisi

For Peace and Understanding

And the work of righteousness shall be peace; and the effect of righteousness quietness and assurance for ever.

—Isaiah 32:17

Sometimes I begin to slip into the illusion that I am in control of my world, Father. I imagine that I can arrange things just the way I like them and that I can create my own peace by making sure everyone and everything follows my plan. Oh, how that house of cards gets blown away in the winds of adversity! How quickly I am reminded that I cannot manufacture peace with manipulation. You are my peace. You are my source of well-being, safety, and security. Apart from you there is no true peace to be had.

For Peace and Understanding

Where there is peace, God is.

—George Herbert

For Peace and Understanding

Lest thou shouldest ponder the path of life, her ways are moveable, that thou canst not know them.

—Proverbs 5:6

Lord,

I seek to understand your will for me, and to follow it with a joyful heart and spirit. Let me feel your presence moving me in the direction you want me to go. Let me be guided in all my ways by your love and kindness. Let me know the power of your grace as you open the right doors for me, and keep me from the things that would bring me sadness and harm. I seek to know your will, Lord, and to live in that will today and always. Amen.

For Peace and Understanding

O that thou hadst hearkened to my commandments!
then had thy peace been as a river,
and thy righteousness as the waves of the sea.

—Isaiah 48:18

Like a river glorious is God's perfect peace,
Over all victorious in its bright increase;
Perfect, yet it floweth fuller every day,
Perfect, yet it groweth deeper all the way.
Ev'ry joy or trial falleth from above,
Traced upon our dial by the sun of love;
We may trust him fuller all for us to do
They who trust him wholly find him wholly true.
Stayed upon Jehovah, hearts are fully blest—
Finding, as he promised, perfect peace and rest.

—Frances Ridley Havergal

For Peace and Understanding

*Glory to God in the highest, and on earth peace,
good will toward men.*

—Luke 2:14

For Peace and Understanding

●━━◆━━●

*H*eavenly Father, be with those who need you today. So many in this world have never felt the peace that passes understanding, the calm and serenity that comes when we turn over our lives to your wise and loving guidance. Instead, they live their lives alone, not realizing you are only an arm's reach from them. For each struggling soul, I pray that you would offer them your boundless mercy and love, helping them to come to know you.

For Peace and Understanding

We find great things are made of little things,
And little things go lessening till at last
Comes God behind them.

—Robert Browning

For Peace and Understanding

Better is a handful with quietness, than both the hands full with travail and vexation of spirit.

—Ecclesiastes 4:6

Dear God,
Drop thy still dews of quietness,
Till all our strivings cease;
Take from our souls the strain and stress,
And let our ordered lives confess
Thy beauty of thy peace.

—John Greenleaf Whittier

For Peace and Understanding

But whoso hearkeneth unto me shall dwell safely,
and shall be quiet from fear of evil.

—Proverbs 1:33

Before prayer
I weave a silence on my lips,
I weave a silence into my mind,
I weave a silence within my heart.
I close my ears to distractions,
I close my eyes to attentions,
I close my heart to temptations.
Calm me O Lord as you stilled the storm,
Still me O Lord, keep me from harm.
Let all the tumult within me cease,
Enfold me Lord in your peace.

—Celtic Traditional

For Peace and Understanding

God, bring peace to the rough places in the world. Bring hope to the hearts that have grown cold and love to the souls that know only violence and despair. Bring wisdom and understanding to those who see around them only chaos. Bring comfort to those who suffer. For you alone can show this world what true and lasting peace is, the peace that is available to us all if we lay down our prejudices and our pride and take up instead love and tolerance. God, bring peace to the dark places of the world, that they may know light.

For Peace and Understanding

*R*enounce all strength, but strength divine,
And peace shall be for ever thine.

—William Cowper

When a man's ways please the Lord,
he maketh even his enemies to be at peace with him.

—Proverbs 16:7

For Peace and Understanding

I will both lay me down in peace, and sleep: for thou, Lord, only makest me dwell in safety.

—Psalm 4:8

O Lord God, who has given us the night for rest, I pray that in my sleep my soul may remain awake to you, steadfastly adhering to your love. As I lay aside my cares to relax and relieve my mind, may I not forget your infinite and unresting care for me. And in this way, let my conscience be at peace, so that when I rise tomorrow, I am refreshed in body, mind, and soul.

—John Calvin

For Happiness

And my soul shall be joyful in the Lord:
it shall rejoice in his salvation.

—Psalm 35:9

For Happiness

He that despiseth his neighbour sinneth: but he that hath mercy on the poor, happy is he.

—Proverbs 14:21

*H*appiness seems made to be shared.

—Jean Racine

For Happiness

But the fruit of the Spirit is love, joy, peace, longsuffering,
gentleness, goodness, faith . . .

—Galatians 5:22

Joy is not gush; joy is not jolliness. Joy is perfect
acquiescence in God's will because the soul delights in
God himself.

—H. W. Webb-Peploe

For Happiness

◆

Almighty God, I keep finding rich nuggets of truth in your word. Here I find that my strength comes not always from holiness or earnestness but from your glory and joy. I've often considered joy a frivolous thing—a good feeling easily swept away by the more important issues of life—but here I discover otherwise. When I find my pleasure in you, dear God, that brings meaning to my whole life. When I exult in your presence each day, I find energy for every task. Strengthen me today, God, with your joy!

For Happiness

I will speak of the glorious honour of thy majesty, and of thy wondrous works.

—Psalm 145:5

If happiness consists in the number of pleasing emotions that occupy our mind—how true is it that the contemplation of nature, which always gives rise to these emotions, is one of the great sources of happiness.

—Thomas Belt

For Happiness

God passes through the thicket of the world, and
wherever his glance falls he turns all things to beauty.

—St. John of the Cross

For Happiness

Not that I speak in respect of want: for I have learned, in whatsoever state I am, therewith to be content.

—Philippians 4:11

I was too ambitious in my deed,
And thought to distance all men in success,
Till God came to me, marked the place and said, "Ill doer, henceforth keep
me within this line, Attempting less than others"—and I stand
And work among Christ's little ones, content.

—Elizabeth Barrett Browning, "Content in Service"

For Happiness

Lord, you are the source of all joy! Regardless of how happy we may feel at any given time, we know happiness is fleeting. Happiness, so dependent on temporary circumstances, is fickle and unpredictable. But joy in you is forever! And so we come to you today, Lord, rejoicing in all you were, all you are, and all you will ever be. Because of you, we rejoice!

For Happiness

Every man according as he purposeth in his heart, so let him give;
not grudgingly, or of necessity: for God loveth a cheerful giver.

—2 Corinthians 9:7

Be it health or be it leisure,
Be it skill we have to give,
Still in spending it for others
Christians only really live.
Not in having or receiving,
But in giving, there is bliss;
He who has no other pleasure
Ever may rejoice in this.

—Author Unknown

For Happiness

Heavenly Father, when I stop for a moment and just think about all the blessings you've showered on me, I'm filled with joy and happiness. I often complain about my problems and focus on the things I wish I had, but in these quiet moments I truly become aware of just how few problems I do have and how much you've given me. Thank you for slowing down my often hectic and crazy life every now and then so I can recognize these moments of pure joy.

For Happiness

The desire of a man is his kindness:
and a poor man is better than a liar.

—Proverbs 19:22

I have wept in the night
For the shortness of sight
That to somebody's need made me blind.
But I never have yet
Felt a tinge of regret
For being a little too kind!

—Author Unknown

For Happiness

Give instruction to a wise man, and he will be yet wiser: teach a just man, and he will increase in learning.

—Proverbs 9:9

I wish you could truly begin the study of God. This must be our delight throughout eternity. It is the happiest and most helpful study that can possibly engage our thoughts. Why cannot we know God without study? Because all knowledge is thus acquired. To learn a thing without study is to forget it. To learn and not use, is also to forget. Life is unhappy to many because they know so little of God. Those who know Him best are most anxious to know more of Him.

—David C. Cook

For Happiness

I am the vine, ye are the branches: He that abideth in me, and I in him, the same bringeth forth much fruit: for without me ye can do nothing.

—John 15:5

Remember, in the first place, that the Vine was the Eastern symbol of Joy. It was its fruit that made glad the heart of man. Yet, however innocent that gladness—for the expressed juice of the grape was the common drink at every peasant's board—the gladness was only a gross and passing thing. This was not true happiness, and the vine of the Palestine vineyards was not the true vine. "Christ was the true Vine." Here, then, is the ultimate source of Joy. Through whatever media it reaches us, all true Joy and Gladness find their source in Christ.

—Henry Drummond

For Happiness

Glory and honour are in his presence;
strength and gladness are in his place.

—1 Chronicles 16:27

Joyful, joyful, we adore thee, God of glory, Lord of love;

hearts unfold like flow'rs before thee,

op'ning to the sun above.

Melt the clouds of sin and sadness,

drive the dark of doubt away;

giver of immortal gladness, fill us with the light of day.

All thy works with joy surround thee,

earth and heav'n reflect thy rays,

stars and angels sing around thee,

center of unbroken praise.

Field and forest, vale and mountain,

flowery meadow, flashing sea,

chanting bird and flowing fountain,

call us to rejoice in thee.

—Henry van Dyke

For Happiness

But whoso keepeth his word, in him verily is the love of God perfected: hereby know we that we are in him.

—1 John 2:5

Joy is love expected;
peace is love in repose;
long-suffering is love enduring;
gentleness is love in society;
goodness is love in action;
faith is love on the battlefield;
meekness is love in school;
and temperance is love in training.

—Dwight L. Moody

For Happiness

Dear God,

I look around and see so many people hurting one another, and it makes my heart heavy and sad. What kind of world are we creating for our children? Why must there be so much hatred and violence and inhumanity? I pray for a way to walk through this world without drowning in sorrow and defeat. I pray for a light to focus upon when all I hear and see is dark and bleak. Help me, God, to focus on the beauty and wonder the world has to offer. Help me recognize the good and the kind and the loving. I pray to see beyond my sadness and despair to the miracles that occur every day, and to not let my disappointment overshadow my hope. Amen.

For Happiness

*Nor height, nor depth, nor any other creature,
shall be able to separate us from the love of God,
which is in Christ Jesus our Lord.*

—Romans 8:39

Your joy surprises me, Lord. Just when I think I have you figured out, something happens that shatters my assumptions. It's then that your joy taps me on the shoulder and takes me on a new journey. Thank you, Lord!

For Happiness

My God, my happiness is my faith, and I'm filled each day with gratitude and awe at the power of your presence and the wonder of your miracles. You have never abandoned me, even when I was in my darkest hours. You have never walked away from me, no matter what sin I've committed. I'm bursting with happiness at the realization that you're my loving, caring, forgiving Father, who is always looking out for me. Amen.

For Happiness

Thou art all fair, my love; there is no spot in thee.

—Song of Solomon 4:7

Where there is charity and wisdom,
there is neither fear nor ignorance.
Where there is patience and humility,
there is neither anger nor vexation.
Where there is poverty and joy,
there is neither greed nor avarice.
Where there is peace and meditation,
there is neither anxiety nor doubt.

—St. Francis of Assisi

For Happiness

Count your blessings, name them one by one:
Count your blessings, see what God hath done.
Count your blessings, name them one by one;
Count your many blessings, see what God hath done.

—Johnson Oatman, Jr.

For Happiness

My love be with you all in Christ Jesus. Amen.

—1 Corinthians 16:24

Loving Father, help us remember the birth of Jesus, that we may share in the song of the angels, the gladness of the shepherds and the wisdom of the wise men. Close the door of hate and open the door of love all over the world. Let kindness come with every gift and good desires with every greeting. Deliver us from evil by the blessing which Christ brings and teach us to be merry with clean hearts.

For Happiness

◆

I celebrate you, dear Lord, and all that you have given me. I'm filled with a sense of pure joy as I look around at the wonderful people and things you have brought into my life. From my friends and family to the place I call home, I've been truly blessed with wonderful things, and I owe all of those good things to you. Thank you for showing me heaven on Earth and for bringing joy into my life each and every day. Amen.

For Happiness

Happy are thy men, and happy are these thy servants, which stand continually before thee, and hear thy wisdom.

—2 Chronicles 9:7

$\mathscr{L}$et us therefore desire nothing else, wish for nothing else, and let nothing please and delight us except our Creator and Redeemer, and Savior, the only true God, who is full of good, who alone is good . . . and from whom, and through whom, and in whom is all mercy, all grace, all glory of all penitents and of the just, and of all the blessed rejoicing in heaven.

—St. Francis of Assisi

For Happiness

But seek ye first the kingdom of God, and his righteousness; and all these things shall be added unto you.

—Matthew 6:33

Lord, may your kingdom come into my heart to sanctify me, nourish me, and purify me. How insignificant is the passing moment to the eye without faith! But how important each moment is to the eye enlightened by faith! How can we deem insignificant anything which has been caused by you? Every moment and every event is guided by you, and so contains your infinite greatness. So, Lord, I glorify you in everything that happens to me. In whatever manner you make me live and die, I am content. Everything is heaven to me, because all my moments manifest your love.

—Jean-Pierre de Caussade, "The Passing Moment"

For Happiness

All praise to Him who now hath turned
My fears to joys, my sighs to song,
My tears to smiles, my sad to glad. Amen.

—Anne Bradstreet

For Happiness

The Lord make his face shine upon thee,
and be gracious unto thee . . .

—Numbers 6:25

For the beauty of the earth,
For the glory of the skies;
For the love which from our birth,
Over and around us lies;
Lord of all, to Thee we raise
This, our hymn of grateful praise.
For the joy of human love,
Brother, sister, parent, child;
Friends on Earth and friends above,
For all gentle thoughts and mild;
Lord of all, to Thee we raise
This, our hymn of grateful praise.

—Folliott S. Pierpont

For Happiness

How fortunate I feel today!
All is well.
Things are working out.
But is it luck . . . or is it your love?
I will assume the latter
And offer words of praise:
Bless your name, Almighty One!

For Happiness

He hath made his wonderful works to be remembered:
the Lord is gracious and full of compassion.

—Psalm 111:4

*H*ow blessed are the good memories, Lord! In fact,
I am beginning to see that my happiness can consist
largely in the looking back. For that I am thankful, as I
lay here, unable for the moment to be active.

For Happiness

That I may publish with the voice of thanksgiving, and tell of all thy wondrous works.

—Psalm 26:7

*L*ord, I can hear your voice in the bubbling brook, see your beauty in the petals of a flower, and feel your gentle breath in the evening breeze and in the soft kiss of a child. Thank you for all of these gifts.

For Happiness

God, you instruct us to come to you for everything we seek, and yet, I feel the sense of discontent that I don't understand and cannot seem to shake. I want nothing more than to fully know the joy that comes from surrendering to your will. I want nothing more than to achieve that sense of inner peace that only comes from being touched by your merciful love and grace. Let me know this joy and this peace today, dear God.

For Happiness

The soul of the sluggard desireth, and hath nothing:
but the soul of the diligent shall be made fat.

—Proverbs 13:4

*L*et us therefore desire nothing else, wish for nothing else, and let nothing please and delight us except our Creator and Redeemer, and Savior.

—St. Francis of Assisi

For Happiness

Delight thyself also in the Lord: and he shall give thee the desires of thine heart.

—Psalm 37:4

*N*one but God can satisfy the longing of the immortal soul; as the heart was made for Him, He only can fill it.

—Richard Trench

For Happiness

To be in Christ is the source of the Christian's life; to be like Christ is the sum of His excellence; to be with Christ is the fullness of his joy.

—Charles Hodge

For Happiness

Lord, how joyful I feel today, for the past is behind me and I'm facing a bright and beautiful future. Thanks to your presence and constant compassion, I have overcome great challenges, and now I feel strong and fully alive as I take on a whole new life. You, dear Lord, have recreated me, and now I truly feel as though my life has meaning and purpose. I'm here for a reason, and I now ask that you reveal that reason to me and let me go out and spread the joy to others. Amen.

For Happiness

$\cdot\!\!-\!\!\blacklozenge\!\!-\!\!\cdot$

Heavenly Father, what can be more joyful than to realize that through you, all things are possible? Even when I'm at the lowest point in my life, I only have to reach out to you, and you take me and lift me up again. Though there is much trouble and hardship in my life right now, my joy is in knowing that you have reserved a place for me in your heavenly kingdom. Thank you, Father.

For Love

Thou shalt not avenge, nor bear any grudge against the children of thy people, but thou shalt love thy neighbour as thyself: I am the Lord.

—Leviticus 19:18

For Love

◆

*H*ow can I love God—the originator and the instigator of all love? If God is love, and he is self-sufficient, how can I possibly show him I love him? By receiving his love.

For Love

$\bullet$ ━ ◆ ━ $\bullet$

Sometimes I get so wrapped up with tending to the stuff of life that I forget to stop and enjoy the fact that you are taking care of me, that you are right here with me, and that your goodness and unfailing love never leaves me. Your presence with me is my greatest need, and that need is met every moment of every day; I don't need to chase after it, go to the store to buy it, repair it, or replace it. I want to stop right now and just relish the blessing of being in your care, dear Shepherd of my life. I love you and want to follow you forever.

For Love

For God so loved the world, that he gave his only begotten Son,
that whosoever believeth in him should not perish,
but have everlasting life.

—John 3:16

I think that the purpose and cause of the
Incarnation [the coming of Jesus] was that God might
illuminate the world by his wisdom and excite it to the
love of himself.

—Peter Abelard

For Love

***

I feel kind of giddy sometimes when I think about the fact that you, the God of the Universe, love me; that you, the one who called forth the wonders of earth and sky, know me by name and care for me. What thoughts! You bowl me over with fresh revelations of your saving love, and I'm glad all over again.

For Love

And though I have the gift of prophecy, and understand all mysteries, and all knowledge; and though I have all faith, so that I could remove mountains, and have not charity, I am nothing.

—1 Corinthians 13:2

Dear God,

Today I pray for a little extra love to get me through the day. I pray to walk in the light of your everlasting and unceasing love, God, for I know that when I stay aligned with your will and purpose for me, life is filled with blessings. I ask for direction, and should I veer off path, that you gently bring me back to where you need me to be. In your loving presence, let me blossom and bloom into the best me I can be, and spread love to everyone I come in contact with. Like a lighthouse beacon guiding boats to the safety of shore, shine your loving light upon me, God, and lead me where you will. Amen.

For Love

Consider Jesus of Nazareth, the most generous-hearted person who ever lived. He never refused a request for help. Great multitudes followed him, and he healed them all. He went out of his way to cross racial and religious barriers. He compassed the whole world in his love.

For Love

As the Father hath loved me, so have I loved you:
continue ye in my love.

—John 15:9

Our Lord does not care so much for the importance of our works as for the love with which they are done.

—Teresa of Avila

For Love

Dear God,

I enjoy being able to freely express my love for you in houses of worship and among other Christians. Thank you, Lord, for the church, where I can praise you and worship you with an open and sincere heart. Let my worship be pleasing to you, not a show for others or a rote exercise of tradition, but a living sacrifice of love to you, holy and acceptable in you sight.

For Love

Jesus, Teacher of patience, Pattern of gentleness,
Prophet of the kingdom of heaven, I adore Thee.

—A Book of Prayers for Students

*They are of those that rebel against the light; they know not the
ways thereof, nor abide in the paths thereof.*

—Job 24:13

How good it is, Almighty One, to bask in the
warmth of your love. To know nothing more is required
than this: receive your good gifts from above.

For Love

For I am persuaded, that neither death, nor life, nor angels, nor principalities, nor powers, nor things present, nor things to come, Nor height, nor depth, nor any other creature, shall be able to separate us from the love of God, which is in Christ Jesus our Lord.

—Romans 8:38–39

Lord,

Love indeed makes the world go around and nothing compares to your love. My prayers today are not just for myself, but for all living things, that we may all feel a little more loved, a little more cherished. So many of us go through life thinking we don't matter. I pray your love awakens them to truly understand, as I do, that every single one of us is precious in your sight. I pray love wins over hate and lightens every dark corner. I pray love dominates the hearts of humans and erases hatred and division. I pray your love serves to bring us together and close the gaps of differences and separation. Love is the greatest miracle, Lord, and I am grateful to experience your love daily. Amen.

For Love

He loveth righteousness and judgment:
the earth is full of the goodness of the Lord.

—Psalm 33:5

*L*ord, since you exist, we exist. Since you are
beautiful, we are beautiful. Since you are good, we are
good. By our existence we honour you. By our beauty
we glorify you. By our goodness we love you.

—Edmund of Abingdon

For Love

O, God of heaven and earth!

You are both the source of and the best object of my love. Your command for me to love you is a wonderful one, and I will willingly say yes to it with a heart full of gladness today. Please grant that I may always love you and that I might learn to love you wholeheartedly. You're more than worthy of all my devotion.

For Love

And thou shalt love the Lord thy God with all thine heart, and with all thy soul, and with all thy might.

—Deuteronomy 6:5

He prayeth best who loveth best all things both great and small; for the dear God who loveth us, he made and loveth all.

—Samuel Taylor Coleridge

For Love

Grace be with all them that love our Lord Jesus Christ in sincerity. Amen.

—Ephesians 6:24

Lord, you are here,
Lord, you are there.
You are wherever we go.
Lord, you guide us,
Lord, you protect us.
You are wherever we go.
Lord, we need you,
Lord, we trust you,
You are wherever we go.
Lord, we love you,
Lord, we praise you,
You are wherever we go.

For Love

I love them that love me;
and those that seek me early shall find me.

—Proverbs 8:17

O most merciful Lord, grant to me thy grace, that it may be with me, and labour with me, and persevere with me even to the end. Grant that I may always desire and will that which is to thee most acceptable, and most dear. Let thy will be mine, and my will ever follow thine, and agree perfectly with it. Grant to me above all things that can be desired, to rest in thee, and in thee to have my heart at peace.

—Thomas à Kempis

For Love

Four stages of growth in Christian maturity
Love of self for self's sake
Love of God for self's sake
Love of God for God's sake
Love of self for God's sake.

—St. Bernard of Clairvaux

For Love

Open wide the window of our spirits, O Lord, and fill us full of light;
Open wide the door of our hearts, that we may receive and entertain thee
with all our powers of adoration and love.

—Christina Rossetti

For Love

*That Christ may dwell in your hearts by faith; that ye,
being rooted and grounded in love . . .*

—Ephesians 3:17

*L*ove is greater than faith, because the end is greater than the means. What is the use of having faith? It is to connect the soul to God. And what is the object of connecting man with God? That he may become like God. But God is Love. Hence, Faith, the means, is in order to Love, the end. Love, therefore, obviously is greater than faith. "If I have all faith, so as to remove mountains, but have not love, I am nothing."

—Henry Drummond

For Love

◆

In your unfailing love, Lord Jesus, you have provided salvation for me. Your sacrifice moves me each time I consider it. Only you have loved me—only you could love me—in this way. Your love has planted the seed of love in my heart that continues to grow. I will never forget the day you showed me your salvation, and I will never stop rejoicing in it. Eternity itself cannot wear out my heart of grateful love for you.

For Love

Owe no man any thing, but to love one another: for he that loveth another hath fulfilled the law.

—Romans 13:8

All the service that weighs an ounce in the sight of God is that which is prompted by love.

—Billy Sunday

For Love

. . . in all human sorrows nothing gives comfort but love and faith.

—Leo Tolstoy, *Anna Karenina*

For Love

Flee also youthful lusts: but follow righteousness,
faith, charity, peace, with them that call on
the Lord out of a pure heart.

—2 Timothy 2:22

Dear Lord,

I've been alone for a while now, and I would love someone special in my life to share my ups and downs and the experiences of being alive with. On my own, I am liable to pick someone who may not be the best for me, so I ask in prayer that you send to me the perfect mate, who is a lover, a friend, a partner, and a confidante. I ask for someone I can trust and lean on and laugh with, and someone who shares my views and values, yet challenges me to always think beyond my own limited vision and be more of myself. Lord, direct my steps to this perfect love, one that is perfect for me in your view. I am ready to love, and to be loved. Amen.

For Love

We praise you, Lord, for eternal life. And we thank you for your love for each one of us. Amen.

O worship the King, all glorious above, O gratefully sing his power and his love.

—Robert Grant

For Love

The kiss of the sun for pardon,
The song of the birds for mirth,
One is nearer God's heart in a garden
Than anywhere else on earth.

—Dorothy Frances Gurney

For Love

Fulfil ye my joy, that ye be like minded, having the same love, being of one accord, of one mind.

—Philippians 2:2

For Love

A new commandment I give unto you, That ye love one another; as I have loved you, that ye also love one another.

—John 13:34

God,

Teach me to walk in love today. With the stressful and hectic nature of life, I find myself giving in to anger, unkindness, and even hatred, and that is not how I want to live or behave. Help me turn to a loving solution for every problem, and to stand in love even when I am surrounded by negativity and confusion. Show me how to always depend on your love, even if at times my own capacity to love others fails me. I ask that I always try to be a loving channel of your presence, and that in the times when I am failing, you come to my aid and remind me of the precious power of love and how much it is needed in this world. Thank you, God. Amen.

For Love

He that loveth not knoweth not God; for God is love.

—1 John 4:8

Count neither the hours nor the seconds
That filled your mind with doubts and fears.
Do not add up unhappy moments,
When pain and hardships brought you to tears.
Regard not days on faded calendars
That marked the passage of your years.
Instead, count heaven's blessings . . .
Grandchildren playing on the floor,
Old friends walking through the door,
White clouds drifting up above,
And, like a faithful timepiece, God's love.

For Love

Grace be with you, mercy, and peace, from God the Father,
and from the Lord Jesus Christ, the Son of the Father,
in truth and love.

—2 John 1:3

Give to the winds thy fears
Hope and be undismayed;
God hears thy sighs and counts thy tears
God shall lift up thy head.
Through waves and clouds and storms,
He gently clears thy way.
Wait thou his time; so shall this night
Soon end in joyous day.
Let us in life, death,
They steadfast truth declare
And publish with our latest breath
Thy love and guardian care.

—Paul Gerhardt, translated by John Wesley

For Love

We cannot in any better manner glorify the Lord and Creator of the universe than that in all things, how small soever they appear to our naked eyes, but which have yet received the gift of life and power of increase, we contemplate the display of his omnificence and perfections with utmost admiration.

—Anton Van Leeuwenhoek

For Love

O love the Lord, all ye his saints: for the Lord preserveth the faithful, and plentifully rewardeth the proud doer.

—Psalm 31:23

Lord, I believe a rest remains,
To all Thy people known;
A rest where pure enjoyment reigns
And thou art loved alone;
A rest where all our soul's desire
Is fixed on things above;
Where fear and sin and grief expire,
Cast out by perfect love.

—Charles Wesley

For Love

But if any man love God, the same is known of him.

—1 Corinthians 8:3

I believe, God, that you give us faith as a means of getting in touch with your love. For once we have that love, we can pass it on to others.

—Henry Drummond

For Love

Like sun that melts the snow,
my soul absorbs the grace
that beats in gentle, healing rays
from some godly place.
Like rain that heals parched earth,
my body drinks the love
that falls in gently, soothing waves
from heaven up above.

For Love

And to love him with all the heart, and with all the understanding, and with all the soul, and with all the strength, and to love his neighbour as himself, is more than all whole burnt offerings and sacrifices.

—Mark 12:33

For the love of God is broader
Than the measure of man's mind.

—F. W. Faber

For Love

God loves each of us as if there was only one of us.

—St. Augustine

For Family and Friends

For my brethren and companions' sakes,
I will now say, Peace be within thee.
—Psalm 122:8

For Family and Friends

True friendship is a knot that angel hands have tied.

—Anonymous

For Family and Friends

So ought men to love their wives as their own bodies.
He that loveth his wife loveth himself.

—Ephesians 5:28

To have and to hold from this day forward, for better for worse, for richer for poorer, in sickness and in health, to love and to cherish, till death us do part.

—*The Book of Common Prayer: Solemnization of Matrimony*

For Family and Friends

Nevertheless let every one of you in particular so love his wife even as himself; and the wife see that she reverence her husband.

—Ephesians 5:33

$\mathcal{M}$arriage does not ask that you completely lose yourself in the other person. Remember, happy individuals make happy couples. Marriage does not demand that you think and act just like one another. Remember, it was your unique qualities that attracted you to each other in the first place. Marriage only requires that each of you becomes not someone else, but more of who you are already, only now you will become who you are together.

For Family and Friends

*God could not be everywhere, and therefore
he created mothers.*

—Jewish Proverb

For Family and Friends

Trust in the Lord, and do good; so shalt thou dwell in the land, and verily thou shalt be fed.

—Psalm 37:3

Do all the good you can,
By all the means you can,
In all the ways you can,
In all the places you can,
At all the times you can,
To all the people you can,
As long as ever you can.

—John Wesley

For Family and Friends

For where two or three are gathered together in my name, there am I in the midst of them.

—Matthew 18:20

*L*ord, I often pray for others when I need to pray with others. Show me the power of shared prayer as I meet with others in your name and in your presence. Amen.

For Family and Friends

God pardons like a mother who kisses the offense into everlasting forgetfulness.

—Henry Ward Beecher

What we love we shall grow to resemble.

—St. Bernard of Clairvaux

For Family and Friends

And now abideth faith, hope, charity, these three; but the greatest of these is charity.

—1 Corinthians 13:13

The sun gives ever; so the earth—
What it can give so much 'tis worth;
The ocean gives in many ways—
Gives baths, gives fishes, rivers, bays;
So, too, the air, it gives us breath
When it stops giving, comes in death.
  Give, give, be always giving;
  Who gives not is not living;
    The more you give
    The more you live.
God's love hath in us wealth unheaped
Only by giving it is reaped;
The body withers, and the mind
Is pent up by a selfish rind.
Give strength, give thought, give deeds, give pelf,
Give love, give tears, and give thyself.
  Give, give, be always giving,
  Who gives not is not living;
    The more we give
    The more we live.

—Author Unknown

For Family and Friends

Comfort ye, comfort ye my people, saith your God.

—Isaiah 40:1

Dear Lord, thank you for healing my heart and bringing joy and meaning back into my life. Thank you for the people who truly care for me. Help me be a soothing and joyful presence in their lives as well. Amen.

For Family and Friends

Sing, O heavens; and be joyful, O earth; and break forth into singing, O mountains: for the Lord hath comforted his people, and will have mercy upon his afflicted.

—Isaiah 49:13

For the promise you unfold with the opening of each day,
I thank you, Lord.
For blessings shared along the way, I thank you, Lord.
For the comfort of our home filled with love to keep us warm,
I thank you, Lord.
For shelter from the winter storm, I thank you, Lord.
For the gifts of peace and grace you grant the family snug within,
I thank you, Lord.
For shielding us from harm and sin, I thank you, Lord.
For the beauty of the snow sparkling in the winter sun,
I thank you, Lord.
For the peace when the day is done, I thank you, Lord.

For Family and Friends

Thou lovest righteousness, and hatest wickedness: therefore God, thy God, hath anointed thee with the oil of gladness above thy fellows.

—Psalm 45:7

There are some of us . . . who think to ourselves, "If I had only been there! How quick I would have been to help the Baby. I would have washed His linen. How happy I would have been to go with the shepherds to see the Lord lying in the manger!" Yes, we would. We say that because we know how great Christ is, but if we had been there at the time, we would have done no better than the people of Bethlehem. . . . Why don't we do it now? We have Christ in our neighbor.

—Martin Luther

For Family and Friends

Jesus answered and said unto him, If a man love me, he will keep my words: and my Father will love him, and we will come unto him, and make our abode with him.

—John 14:23

I read within a poet's book
A word that starred the page,
"Stone walls do not a prison make,
Nor iron bars a cage."
Yes, that is true, and something more:
You'll find, where'er you roam,
That marble floors and gilded walls
Can never make a home.
But every house where Love abides
And Friendship is a guest,
Is surely home, and home, sweet home;
For there the heart can rest.

—Henry Van Dyke

For Family and Friends

He that loveth pureness of heart, for the grace of his lips the king shall be his friend.

—Proverbs 22:11

To love for the sake of being loved is human, but to love for the sake of loving is angelic.

—Alphonse de Lamartine

For Family and Friends

I have been young, and now am old; yet have I not seen the
righteous forsaken, nor his seed begging bread.

—Psalm 37:25

I believe in one God and no more, and I hope for
happiness beyond this life. I believe in the equality of
man; and I believe that religious duties consist in doing
justice, loving mercy, and endeavoring to make our
fellow creatures happy.

—Thomas Paine

For Family and Friends

*With the merciful thou wilt shew thyself merciful;
with an upright man thou wilt shew thyself upright;*

—Psalm 18:25

Here is my creed. I believe in one God, Creator of the Universe. That he governs it by his Providence. That he ought to be worshipped. That the most acceptable service we render him is doing good to his other children. That the soul of Man is immortal, and will be treated with justice in another life respecting its conduct in this.

—Benjamin Franklin

For Family and Friends

He hath filled the hungry with good things;
and the rich he hath sent empty away.

—Luke 1:53

God, we thank you for this food
for the hands that planted it
for the hands that tended it
for the hands that harvested it
for the hands that prepared it
for the hands that provided it
and for the hands that served it.
And we pray for those without enough food
in your world and in our land of plenty.

For Family and Friends

My little children, let us not love in word,
neither in tongue; but in deed and in truth.

—1 John 3:18

I love little children, and it is not a slight thing
when they, who are fresh from God, love us.

—Charles Dickens

For Family and Friends

The liberal soul shall be made fat:
and he that watereth shall be watered also himself.

—Proverbs 11:25

*L*ord, thank you for bringing others into our lives to help us heal. We appreciate how much they aid us. Please remind us to thank them for reaching out to us. Thank you for extending your love to us through them. Amen.

For Family and Friends

Dear God,

I come to you today giving thanks for all the blessings you've bestowed upon my family. Even through the challenges, your presence has served to remind us we can get through anything with you to lead us. I am forever grateful for the love and grace and mercy you've continued to show us, and for the harder lessons we all have struggled through and learned from. Knowing we have the love of God to light the way has been the glue that has held us all together. Thank you, God. Amen.

For Family and Friends

With gladness and rejoicing shall they be brought:
they shall enter into the king's palace.

—Psalm 45:15

Heavenly Father, I am glad to have even just one companion, but you have sent me many more! I thank you for my friends and family. I am happy to have so many shoulders on which I can lean. Amen.

For Family and Friends

Let thy mercy, O Lord, be upon us, according as we hope in thee.

—Psalm 33:22

Father, it's to you we come,
To pray for loved ones and for friends;
You offer mercy, grace, and peace,
And healing love that never ends.

For Family and Friends

The Lord will give strength unto his people;
the Lord will bless his people with peace.

—Psalm 29:11

Heavenly Father, we are thankful for family. Please bring our family together in happiness. Help us see everything as your children do: with wonder and awe. Glorious are your creations! Thank you for creating us. We love our family. We love you. Amen.

For Family and Friends

*And I heard a great voice out of heaven saying, Behold, the
tabernacle of God is with men, and he will dwell with them,
and they shall be his people, and God himself shall be with them,
and be their God.*

—Revelation 21:3

*P*lease be with us, Lord, when pain strikes us or
those we love. Please watch over us when our bodies
are stricken. Amen and amen.

For Family and Friends

And he brought forth his people with joy,
and his chosen with gladness . . .
—Psalm 105:43

Beloved Lord,

I pray today for my family, not only the family that shares my DNA but also those who share my faith. As you know, families are complicated, and I've told you plenty about my daily problems with this one or that one. Expectations run high. Wounds run deep. There are dysfunctions that only you can unravel, and so I ask you to bring your wisdom and power into those situations. And I also pray for those caring friends who have gathered around me as a second family. Thank you for their supports, and I ask you to support them in their various needs. Let love reign in my home and in my heart. This is my deepest prayer. Amen.

For Family and Friends

Father God, thank you for those angelic persons who bring healing. We will try to mimic their ways.

For Family and Friends

Bless to me, O God, the earth beneath my feet,
Bless to me, O God, the path whereon I go,
Bless to me, O God, the people whom I meet,
Today, tonight and tomorrow.

—Celtic Blessing

*E*very child born into the world is a new thought of God, an ever fresh and radiant possibility.

—Kate Douglas Wiggin

For Family and Friends

That our sons may be as plants grown up in their youth;
that our daughters may be as corner stones,
polished after the similitude of a palace . . .

—Psalm 144:12

Dear God, from whom every family receives its true name, I pray for all the members of my family; for those who are growing up, that they may increase in wisdom and love; for those facing changes, that they may meet them with hope; for those who are weak, that they may find strength; for those with heavy burdens, that they may carry them lightly; for those who are old and frail, that they may grow in faith.

—Anonymous

For Family and Friends

Behold, how good and how pleasant it is for
brethren to dwell together in unity!

—Psalm 133:1

*B*less our homes, dear God, that we cherish the
daily bread before there is none, discover each other
before we leave on our separate ways, and enjoy each
other for what we are, while we have time to do so.

—A Prayer from Hawaii (adapted)

For Family and Friends

The curse of the Lord is in the house of the wicked:
but he blesseth the habitation of the just.

—Proverbs 3:33

Lord, behold our family here assembled. We thank you for this place in which we dwell, for the love that unites us, for the peace accorded us this day, for the hope with which we expect the morrow; for the health, the work, the food and the bright skies that make our lives delightful; for our friends in all parts of the earth. Amen.

—Robert Louis Stevenson

For Family and Friends

The God of my mercy shall prevent me:
God shall let me see my desire upon mine enemies.

—Psalm 59:10

Teach me to feel another's woe,
To hide the fault I see;
That mercy I to others show,
That mercy show to me.

—Alexander Pope

For Family and Friends

•◆•

Dear God,
You don't have to worry about me. I always look both ways.

—Melanie, age 7

For Family and Friends

May God grant you many years to live,
For surely he must be knowing
The earth has angels all too few
And heaven's overflowing!

—Traditional Irish Blessing

For Family and Friends

Now, my son, the Lord be with thee; and prosper thou, and build the house of the Lord thy God, as he hath said of thee.

—1 Chronicles 22:11

Bless this little one of so few days.

May he be prosperous in all his ways.

Healthy in body and mind, growing strong and kind.

Bless this little one through all his days.

Hush, my dear, lie still and slumber,

Holy angels guard thy bed!

Heavenly blessings without number

Gently falling on thy head.

—Isaac Watts

For Family and Friends

A wise son maketh a glad father:
but a foolish man despiseth his mother.

—Proverbs 15:20

Thank you, God, for giving me the blessing of a mother who is more than just a caregiver. She is my best friend and the one I know I can count on when no one else believes in me.

For Family and Friends

For the Lord God is a sun and shield:
the Lord will give grace and glory: no good thing will he
withhold from them that walk uprightly.

—Psalm 84:11

*I*nto thy hands, O Father and Lord, we commend this night, ourselves, our families and friends, all those we love and those who love us, all folk rightly believing, and all who need thy pity and protection: light us with thy holy grace, and suffer us never to be separated from thee, O Lord in Trinity, God everlasting.

—St. Edmund Rich, Archbishop of Canterbury

For Family and Friends

$\mathcal{A}$s I go through this day, help me to be sensitive to the fears and cares of my fellow workers. Remind me not to add my grievances and burdens to their own.

—Anonymous

For Guidance

I will instruct thee and teach thee in the way which
thou shalt go: I will guide thee with mine eye.

—Psalm 32:8

For Guidance

The meek will he guide in judgment:
and the meek will he teach his way.

—Psalm 25:9

Whenever you take a journey—whether across town to a familiar home or across the country to a new place—remember to take an angel with you. The angel will guide your path, watch your steps, and keep you company all along the way.

For Guidance

Hear instruction, and be wise, and refuse it not.

—Proverbs 8:33

There are joys which long to be ours. God sends ten thousand truths, which come about us like birds seeking inlet; but we are shut up to them, and so they bring us nothing, but sit and sing awhile upon the roof and then fly away.

—Henry Ward Beecher, *Life Thoughts* (1858)

For Guidance

Thou shalt guide me with thy counsel,
and afterward receive me to glory.

—Psalm 73:24

*H*ow often we look upon God as our last and feeblest resource! We go to him because we have nowhere else to go. And then we learn that the storms of life have driven us, not upon the rocks, but into the desired haven.

—George MacDonald

For Guidance

To give light to them that sit in darkness and in the shadow of death, to guide our feet into the way of peace.

—Luke 1:79

We must wait for God, long, meekly, in the wind and wet, in the thunder and lightning, in the cold and dark. Wait, and he will come. He never comes to those who do not wait. He does not go their road. When he comes, go with him, but go slowly, fall a little behind; when he quickens his pace, be sure of it before you quicken yours. But when he slackens, slacken at once; and do not be slow only, but silent, very silent, for he is God.

—Frederick W. Faber

For Guidance

And art confident that thou thyself art a guide of the blind,
a light of them which are in darkness . . .

—Romans 2:19

When you are in the dark, listen, and God will give you a
very precious message for someone else when you get into
the light.

—Oswald Chambers

For Guidance

The Lord is my shepherd; I shall not want.

—Psalm 23:1

Savior, like a shepherd lead us,
Much we need thy tender care;
In thy pleasant pastures feed us,
For our use thy folds prepare.
Blessed Jesus, blessed Jesus,
Thou hast bought us, thine we are.
Blessed Jesus, blessed Jesus,
Thou hast bought us, thine we are.

—Dorothy A. Thrupp

For Guidance

*And he took them up in his arms, put his hands upon them,
and blessed them.*

—Mark 10:16

May the road rise to meet you.
May the wind be always at your back.
May the sun shine warm upon your face;
The rains fall soft upon your fields
And, until we meet again,
May God hold you in the palm of his hand.

—Gaelic Blessing

For Guidance

He shall drink of the brook in the way:
therefore shall he lift up the head.

—Psalm 110:7

*M*ove our hearts with the calm, smooth flow of your grace. Let the river of your love run through our souls. May my soul be carried by the current of your love, towards the wide, infinite ocean of heaven. Stretch out my heart with your strength, as you stretch out the sky above the earth. Smooth out any wrinkles of hatred or resentment. Enlarge my soul that it may know more fully your truth.

For Guidance

That ye be not slothful, but followers of them who through faith and patience inherit the promises.

—Hebrews 6:12

Teach us, good Lord, to serve thee as thou deservest. To give and not to count the cost: To fight and not to heed the wounds: To toil and not to seek for rest: To labour and not to ask for any reward save that of knowing that we do thy will.

—St. Ignatius Loyola

For Guidance

We ought to help one another by our advice,
and yet more by our good examples.

—Brother Lawrence,
The Practice of the Presence of God (1958)

For Guidance

Teach me, and I will hold my tongue: and cause me to understand wherein I have erred.

—Job 6:4

Teach me, teach me, dearest Jesus
In thine own sweet loving, way,
All the lessons of perfection
I must practice day by day.
Teach me meekness, dearest Jesus,
Of Thine own the counterpart;
Not in words and actions only,
But the meekness of the heart.
Teach, Humility, sweet Jesus
To this poor, proud heart of mine,
Which yet wishes, O my Jesus,
To be modeled after Thine.

—Reverend F. X. Lasance

For Guidance

Dear Lord,

I need you to shepherd me through life. I know how easily I can go astray, and I know I need your rod and staff to keep me headed in the right direction. I don't even know what the right direction is, but I trust you to lead me. Green pastures, still waters—I am grateful for the blissful moments you provide, but most of all I thank you for your presence beside me, helping me find my way. With your guidance, I will live each day for your name's sake.

For Guidance

I will teach you by the hand of God: that which is with the Almighty will I not conceal.

—John 27:11

O Word of God Incarnate,
O Wisdom from on high,
O Truth unchanged, unchanging,
O Light of our dark sky:
We praise thee for the radiance
That from the hallowed page,
A lantern to our footsteps,
Shines on from age to age.

— "O Word of God Incarnate"

For Guidance

The dawn of a new day brings new possibilities and challenges. We hope they'll all be good ones, but we know they won't, and that's where God comes in.

For Guidance

He restoreth my soul: he leadeth me in the paths of righteousness for his name's sake.

—Psalm 23:3

Immortal love, forever full
forever flowing free,
forever shared, forever whole,
a never ebbing sea.
Through him the first fond prayers said,
our lips of childhood frame;
the last low whispers of our dead
are burdened by his name.
O Lord and master of us all,
whate'er our name or sign,
we own thy sway, we hear thy call
we test our lives by thine.

—John Greenleaf Whittier

For Guidance

*And the Lord went before them by day in a pillar of a cloud,
to lead them the way; and by night in a pillar of fire,
to give them light; to go by day and night . . .*

—Exodus 13:21

O most merciful Redeemer, friend, and brother;
may we know Thee more clearly,
love Thee more dearly,
and follow Thee more nearly,
day by day.

—Richard of Chichester

For Guidance

I beseech you therefore, brethren, by the mercies of God, that ye present your bodies a living sacrifice, holy, acceptable unto God, which is your reasonable service.

—Romans 12:1

The greatest burden that we have to carry in life is self. The most difficult thing we have to manage is self. . . . In laying off your burdens therefore, the first one you must get rid of is yourself. You must hand yourself and all your inward experiences, your temptations, your temperament, your . . . feelings all over into the care and keeping of our God. And leave them there. He made you, He understands you, He knows how to manage you, and you must trust Him to do it.

—Hannah Whitall Smith

For Guidance

Sweet souls around us watch us still,
Press nearer to our side;
Into our thoughts, into our prayers,
With gentle helpings glide.

—Harriet Beecher Stowe, "The Other World"

For Guidance

He is wise in heart, and mighty in strength: who hath hardened himself against him, and hath prospered?

—Job 9:4

God's might to direct me.
God's power to protect me.
God's wisdom for my learning.
God's eye for my discerning.
God's ear for my hearing.
God's word for my clearing.

—St. Patrick

For Guidance

For the wages of sin is death; but the gift of God is eternal life through Jesus Christ our Lord.

—Romans 6:23

Father, this morning I woke up, and the gift of life was still within me. What a privilege! I don't want to lose wonder of it for even one day. So help me to live with purpose and joy, not waiting for what today might bring me, but rather looking for opportunities to be and do all that you've created me for. And, most of all, thank you for being with me in each moment, showing me the way of abundant living.

For Guidance

For he shall give his angels charge over thee,
to keep thee in all thy ways.

—Psalm 91:11

Thank you for the unseen hands that guide my way.
Thank you for the eyes that watch my step. Thank you
for the care that keeps me safe, even when the angels
are incognito. Thank you for the trouble I have missed
even though I never saw it coming. Every visible thing
in the world is under the charge of an angel.

—St. Augustine

For Guidance

Even there shall thy hand lead me,
and thy right hand shall hold me.

—Psalm 139:10

God, I am a child no longer, yet I still know the need to have someone take me by the hand and lead me out of this scary place. Throughout my life you've sent those people to me, and together we have found the way. Bless those angels, Lord. May they find the hands to hold when they need them. Amen.

For Guidance

Hold up my goings in thy paths, that my footsteps slip not.

—Psalm 17:5

O may thy spirit guide my feet
In ways of righteousness;
Make every path of duty straight,
And plain before my face.
Amen.

—Joachim Neander

For Guidance

If I am right, Thy grace impart,
Still in the right to stay;
If I am wrong, oh teach my heart
To find that better way.

—Alexander Pope

For Guidance

Keep me at evening,
Keep me at morning,
Keep me at noon,
I am tired,
Astray and stumbling, shield me from sin.

—Celtic Traditional

For Guidance

Shew me thy ways, O Lord; teach me thy paths.

—Psalm 25:4

When my way is drear, precious Lord, linger near.

When the day is almost gone,

Hear my cry, hear my call,

Hold my hand, lest I fall,

Precious Lord, take my hand, lead me home.

For Guidance

*Sing unto him, sing psalms unto him,
talk ye of all his wondrous works.*

—1 Chronicles 16:9

There is much to drag us back, O Lord: empty pursuits, trivial pleasures, unworthy cares. There is much to frighten us away: pride that makes us reluctant to accept help; cowardice that recoils from sharing your suffering; anguish at the prospect of confessing our sins to you. But you are stronger than all these forces. We call you our redeemer and saviour because you redeem us from our empty, trivial existence, you save us from our foolish fears. This is your work, which you have completed and will continue to complete every moment.

—Søren Kierkegaard

For Guidance

But the path of the just is as the shining light,
that shineth more and more unto the perfect day.

—Proverbs 4:18

Pray without ceasing, let your love illumine the skies
That the darkness of man may drop away
And only the light of God show through.
Pray unto the Holy, with all your heart and soul
Pray for the shining light of guidance
That your path may be glorious with love.

—St. Augustine

For Guidance

Angel of God, my guardian dear,
To whom God's love commits me here,
Ever this day, be at my side,
To light and guard, rule and guide.
Amen.

—Traditional Prayer

For Guidance

Teach me to do thy will; for thou art my God: thy spirit is good; lead me into the land of uprightness.

—Psalm 143:10

Too often, Lord, I make my own plans and forget about yours. I think I know what's best for me, and I set out my goals accordingly. But now I see that this isn't just ungodly, it's not smart. What do I know, compared to you? Do I really expect that I can make wise decisions independent from you? My creator, you made me! You know how I function best! Besides that, you know the rest of the world as well, and what effect I can have on it. So, Lord, right here and now, I acknowledge you. Be my guide through life. Make my paths straight.

For Guidance

Lead me in thy truth, and teach me: for thou art the God of my salvation; on thee do I wait all the day.

—Psalm 25:5

O gracious and holy Father,
Give us wisdom to perceive you,
intelligence to understand you,
diligence to seek you,
patience to wait for you,
eyes to see you,
a heart to meditate on you,
and a life to proclaim you,
through the power of the spirit of Jesus Christ our Lord.

—St. Benedict

For Guidance

Trust the past to God's mercy, the present to God's love,
and the future to God's providence.

—St. Augustine

Whatever I have built in my life, O God, it's because of you. Whatever home I have, whatever career I've established, whatever fortune I've amassed, whatever relationships I treasure—it's all because you have guided me, I owe it all to you. Thank you for these things, and please give me opportunities to tell the next generation of your love and power.

For Guidance

◆

Lord of light, shine your presence deep into my life. Enlighten my heart, and show me the way you want me to go. As I weigh my options, I try to figure out where each path will lead, but it's hard for me to see clearly. Give me your wisdom. Help me understand what's most important to you. Let me see though the guises of deceivers, and let me enjoy the beautiful visage of truth. I want your spirit to radiate through me and outward to others. Let me shine for you.

For Guidance

I feel as if I'm blind right now, My Lord. I feel as if I'm in total darkness. This is uncharted territory for me. I can imagine this road leading to great success or dismal failure. I don't know what to do. So please, Lord, I beg you, guide me through this terrain. Let me see where you want me to go. I want to be obedient to your will.

For Forgiveness

Look upon mine affliction and my pain;
and forgive all my sins.

—Psalm 25:18

For Forgiveness

I have waited for thy salvation, O Lord.

—Genesis 49:18

Come, Thou long-expected Jesus,
Born to set thy people free;
From our fears and sin release us;
Let us find our rest in thee.

—Charles Wesley

For Forgiveness

But if ye forgive not men their trespasses, neither will your Father forgive your trespasses.

—Matthew 6:15

Jesus Christ will be the Lord of all or he will not be Lord of all.

—St. Augustine

For Forgiveness

*And when ye stand praying, forgive,
if ye have ought against any: that your Father
also which is in heaven may forgive you your trespasses.*

—Mark 11:25

Lord,

I am having trouble forgiving someone who betrayed me.
I know that it would be what you want, but I don't have
the strength to let it go. Please help me look deep within
to find that strength and to allow myself and this other
person the gift of forgiveness. You have always forgiven
me my mistakes and shortcomings, help me to do the
same for someone else and release us both from the
bondage of anger and disappointment. Amen.

For Forgiveness

What does redemption mean? To me, it means to be cleansed and renewed, free from burdens of my past mistakes. God, your forgiveness brings me that clarity and redemption, and that renewal of my spirit. Your grace frees me from the bonds of the past that weighed me down and made my life feel so heavy. I ask in prayer today that you work with me to free those who I've kept in the bondage of their sins against me. Help me forgive them, not just because it will set me free of anger and pain in the process, but also because you have already forgiven them. We all sin. We all deserve to be made clean and whole again.

For Forgiveness

And be ye kind one to another, tenderhearted, forgiving one another, even as God for Christ's sake hath forgiven you.

—Ephesians 4:32

Christ is no Moses, no exactor, no giver of laws, but a giver of grace, a Savior; he is infinite mercy and goodness, freely and bountifully giving to us.

—Martin Luther

For Forgiveness

Judge not, and ye shall not be judged: condemn not, and ye shall not be condemned: forgive, and ye shall be forgiven . . .

—Luke 6:37

Dear God,

Why is it often the people closest to us that hurt us the most? Today I ask for the strength to deal with difficult people in the way you would want me to. Today I ask for the ability to find it in my heart to forgive them their trespasses, as I would hope they'd forgive mine. Today I ask for enough love to look beyond their problems and see them as you see them, as human beings deserving of love and care, even if I have to do it from a distance. Help me to forgive and move on, God. Amen.

For Forgiveness

He that covereth his sins shall not prosper: but whoso confesseth and forsaketh them shall have mercy.

—Proverbs 28:13

Lord, I confess to you,
sadly, my sin;
all I am, I tell to you,
all I have been.
Purge all my sin away,
wash clean my soul
this day;
Lord, make me clean.
Then all is peace and
light this soul within;
thus shall I walk with you,
loved though unseen.
Leaning on you, my God,
guided along the road,
nothing between!

—Horatius Bonar

For Forgiveness

Blessed is he whose transgression is forgiven, whose sin is covered. Blessed is the man unto whom the LORD imputeth not iniquity, and in whose spirit there is no guile.

—Psalm 32:1–2

Dear Lord,

I've been able to forgive others who have hurt me, but why can't I forgive myself? I've made so many bad choices in life, and now I feel as though they're catching up with me. I know that you forgive me of any transgressions, but please help me today to let go of the regret and sorrow over things I didn't do right, and choices I made in haste. Help me release the grip of anger for my sins, because it's only serving to make me unhappy and sick inside. I long to be set free of the past, and face a fresh future with you beside me to guide my ways. Help me forgive the one person in my life that needs it most, Lord: myself. Thank you. Amen.

For Forgiveness

God will either give you what you ask, or something far better.

—Robert Murray McCheyne

As I seek your forgiveness today, heavenly Father, let it be with a sincere heart that humbly listens to your voice of loving correction. Help me not be proud or presumptuous nor, on the other hand, self-condemning and hopeless. May I come ready to receive your forgiveness and prepared to walk in a new direction that leads to wholeness.

For Forgiveness

And my soul shall be joyful in the Lord:
it shall rejoice in his salvation.

—Psalm 35:9

Lord, dismiss us with thy blessing,
Hope, and comfort from above;
Let us each, thy peace possessing,
Triumph in redeeming love.

—Robert Hawker

For Forgiveness

Be it known unto you therefore, men and brethren, that
through this man is preached unto you the forgiveness of sins:
And by him all that believe are justified from all things, from
which ye could not be justified by the law of Moses.

—Acts 13:38–39

God,

I ask in prayer for your forgiveness. I've not been the most loving and kind person lately, and I've treated people terribly as a result. I plan to reach out to each and every one of them and ask their forgiveness, but first I come to you in hopes that you will help me be a better person, a more loving and caring friend, and someone who treats others as I'd like to be treated. Please take away the defects in me that cause me to do harm to others, and strengthen the good qualities I have. I am a loving person, but when life backs me into a corner, I know I can be awful. Please forgive me and empower me to make better choices in the future and be the person you want me to be. Amen.

For Forgiveness

But I have trusted in thy mercy;
my heart shall rejoice in thy salvation.

—Psalm 13:5

God that madest earth and heaven,
darkness and light
Who the day for toil has given
For rest the night
Guard us waking, guard us sleeping
and when we die
May we in thy mighty keeping
All peaceful lie.

—R. Heber

For Forgiveness

Even as I look to you for forgiveness today, Lord God, please grant me a strengthened heart to follow through with true repentance. Your forgiveness is given freely because of your great love. Please fill me with a reciprocating love that wants to draw near to you and to your ways. Give me a heart that is not at ease in sinful habits and paths, a heart that returns to you and remains with you.

For Forgiveness

Love thou thy fellow man!
   He may have sinned, One proof indeed,
He is thy fellow, reach thy hand
   And help him in his need!
Love thou thy fellow man. He may
   Have wronged thee—then, the less excuse
Thou hast for wronging him. Obey
   What he has dared refuse!
Love thou thy fellow man—for, be
   His life a light or heavy load,
No less he needs the love of thee
   To help him on his road.

—James Whitcomb Riley

For Forgiveness

For thou, Lord, art good, and ready to forgive; and plenteous in mercy unto all them that call upon thee.

—Psalm 86:5

Dear God,

Help me forgive my children for their mistakes, and understand that they are small and not yet mature in their behaviors. They don't misbehave because they are bad, but because they are children, and I ask that you always remind me that anything they break or mess up is not as important as making sure they know I love them. Please give me the patience to deal with them when they are bad, and the wisdom to let go of things that are truly not that important, even if I am angry or disappointed. Remind me, God, that I won't have my precious little ones forever, and to cherish and enjoy them while I can. Amen.

For Forgiveness

He that followeth after righteousness and mercy findeth life,
righteousness, and honour.

—Proverbs 21:21

The Lord hath spoken peace to my soul,
He hath blessed me abundantly,
Hath pardoned my sins;
He hath shown me great mercy and saved me
by his love.
I will sing of his goodness and mercy while
I live,
And ever, forever will praise his holy name.
O how sweet to trust in God,
And to know your sins forgiven,
To believe his precious word,
And be guided by his love.
Therefore goodness and mercy,
Shall follow me all the days of my life.
Amen.

—C.E. Leslie

For Forgiveness

◆

I know that my sin affects me, dear Father. It changes me. It mucks up my heart and causes me to behave in a sort of independence from you that goes from bad to worse. Not only do I need your forgiveness right now, but I also need a renewed heart and mind. Please wash away the grime of sin I've allowed to accumulate. I want to see things from your perspective again. I want to care about what is right and true and good. I want to be in close fellowship with you once more. Oh, how good it is to be renewed.

For Forgiveness

＊◆＊

The story is told that someone asked Martin Luther (1483-1546) if he "felt" that he had been forgiven. His reply: "No, but I'm as sure as there's a God in Heaven. For feelings come, and feelings go, and feelings are deceiving. My warrant is the Word of God, naught else is worth believing."

—Martin Luther

For Forgiveness

The world will judge our doctrines by our deeds.

—Author Unknown

For Forgiveness

Who hath delivered us from the power of darkness, and hath translated us into the kingdom of his dear Son: In whom we have redemption through his blood, even the forgiveness of sins.

—Colossians 1:13–14

Lord,

There's a saying that implies we should forgive and forget, but there are some things I just don't think I can forget. Certain people have hurt me deeply, and I don't want their toxic presence in my life anymore. I ask in prayer that you help me come to a place inside my heart where I can truly forgive them of their sins, and let go of them to make way for healing and peace. I no longer want to live in anger and regret, nor do I want to hold on to people who simply are not good for my happiness. Please show me the way to completely forgive, and then to lovingly close the door so that I can begin to become whole again. Amen.

For Forgiveness

If ye forsake the Lord, and serve strange gods,
then he will turn and do you hurt, and consume you,
after that he hath done you good.

—Joshua 24:20

God, when things go wrong, we usually blame you first. Forgive us for even considering that you would deliberately hurt one of your very own children. What could you possibly have to gain? Thank you for your presence, and please forgive our many sins.

For Forgiveness

He is a loving, tender hand, full of sympathy and compassion.

—Dwight L. Moody

For Forgiveness

But that ye may know that the Son of man hath power upon earth to forgive sins, (he said unto the sick of the palsy,) I say unto thee, Arise, and take up thy couch, and go into thine house.

—Luke 5:24

Dear God

I don't come in prayer to you to ask for total forgiveness, even though I know you do forgive me my sins and mistakes. I ask that in addition to your merciful grace, you also help me to learn from my experience and glean wisdom from my interactions with the people I need to forgive, or need forgiveness from. Without this understanding, I fear I will repeat the same patterns in the future. Forgive me, God, then help me to forgive. But then, please, help me to increase my wisdom and come to a place in life where I don't keep repeating the same mistakes over and over again. Amen.

For Forgiveness

Thou hast also given me the shield of thy salvation:
and thy gentleness hath made me great.

—2 Samuel 22:36

Dear Lord and Father of humankind,
Forgive our foolish ways;
Reclothe us in our rightful mind,
In purer lives Thy service find,
In deeper reverence, praise.

—John Greenleaf Whittier

For Forgiveness

To err is human, to forgive divine.

—Alexander Pope

God, I am not perfect. I continue to sin and make mistakes. Sometimes I do things that I am not proud of, things that leave me with nothing but a sense of shame and guilt. I often make lousy decisions. I know it is human nature, but I aspire to be more like you in all my ways. It helps me to know that you forgive me of my shortcomings, but I still pray for the wisdom, strength, and fortitude your love provides. I understand life is about progress, not perfection, God. May I always do better, but when I fall short, thank you for forgiving me.

For Forgiveness

Truly my soul waiteth upon God: from him cometh my salvation.

—Psalm 62:1

*H*e that cannot forgive others, breaks the bridge over which he himself must pass if he would ever reach heaven, for everyone has need to be forgiven.

—George Herbert

For Forgiveness

Restore unto me the joy of thy salvation;
and uphold me with thy free spirit.

—Psalm 51:12

*H*ave thine own way, Lord! Have thine own way! Wounded and weary, help me I pray! Power, all power, surely is thine! Touch me and heal me, Savior divine!

—Adelaide A. Pollard

For Forgiveness

Come, ye disconsolate, where'er ye languish;
Come, at the shrine of God fervently kneel;
Here bring your wounded hearts; here tell your anguish;
Earth has no sorrow that heaven cannot heal.

—Thomas Moore

For Forgiveness

⬥

The Lord knoweth the days of the upright: and their inheritance shall be for ever. They shall not be ashamed in the evil time: and in the days of famine they shall be satisfied.

—Psalm 37:18–19

Lord,

Help me to let go of the chains that bind me to the people I cannot seem to forgive. I pray for strength and wisdom to understand that their sins against me were because of their own deep fears. I pray for the guidance to cut the cord that attaches me to them in anger and the desire for revenge. Teach me to forgive others, Lord, as you forgive me, and to release the poison of resentment that takes away my peace and serenity. Teach me to be a better person and to recognize my own humanity in others, even as I remove their presence from my life. Amen.

For Forgiveness

Shew us thy mercy, O Lord, and grant us thy salvation.

—Psalm 85:7

God grant you many and happy years,
Till when the last has crowned you
The dawn of endless day appears,
And heaven is shining round you!

—Oliver Wendell Holmes

For Forgiveness

Thou hast granted me life and favour,
and thy visitation hath preserved my spirit.

—Job 10:12

Lord God, I kneel before you, and you alone.

I'm sorry for the times I've mistakenly

Credited someone else or something else

For your miraculous work.

How could an angel, a preacher, a friend

Impart your healing power, unless

You were behind it all,

Inspiring, instructing, empowering?

I thank you for the ones you use

On this earth and in your heaven

To help me heal.

Lord God, I kneel before you, and you alone.

Amen

For Forgiveness

If I actually sat down one day and counted how many times I judged another person for something they said or did, I would have one long list. Why is it so easy to judge others, often for things I myself say or do all the time? I guess it's easier to see my faults in someone else, reflected back to me. God, help me to stop judging, and start forgiving. Usually people don't even know they are offending me, or hurting my feelings, and I can always choose to respond differently. Inspire me, God, to have more patience and compassion with people. I think the world would be a much nicer place if we all stopped being so judgmental. Let it begin with me.

For Forgiveness

Behold, I send you forth as sheep in the midst of wolves: be ye therefore wise as serpents, and harmless as doves.

—Matthew 10:16

If I have wounded any soul today,
If I have caused one foot to go astray,
If I have walked in my own willful way,
Dear Lord, forgive!
If I have uttered idle words or vain,
If I have turned aside from want or pain,
Lest I myself shall suffer through the strain,
Dear Lord, forgive!
Forgive the sins I have confessed to Thee;
Forgive the secret sins I do not see;
O guide me, love me and my keeper be,
Dear Lord, Amen.

—C. Maude Battersby

For Forgiveness

◆

*H*eavenly Father, I need to understand that forgiveness is not dependent on my feelings, but rather on a determination of my will. Help me form a few well-chosen words of forgiveness. Amen

◆

*S*in is like a parasite on our spirit, drawing life out of us as it grows ever larger. That's why the sooner we're rid of it, the better we'll be.

For Forgiveness

*L*ord God, the words "I'm sorry" and "forgive me" have got to be the most powerful in our vocabulary. May these phrases ever be poised on my lips, ready to do their work of release and restoration. Let your healing balm wash over me, as I both grant and receive the freedom that forgiveness brings.

For Forgiveness

A man's pride shall bring him low:
but honour shall uphold the humble in spirit.

—Proverbs 29:23

An apology
Is a friendship preserver,
Is often a debt of honor,
Is never a sign of weakness,
Is an antidote for hatred,
Costs nothing but one's pride,
Always saves more than it costs,
Is a device needed in every home.

—Author Unknown

For Forgiveness

＊◆＊

God of grace, I can claim no merit of my own.
There is no reason for you to forgive my sin,
other than your great love for me. I have made
bad choices that have hurt others; I'm well aware
of this. But I throw myself on the mercy of your
court, and I find that you are rich in mercy. You
forgive my sin, you heal my heart, and you bring
me into an exciting kinship with you. This is not
my doing, it's yours, and I thank you for it. My
heart overflows with gratitude for your grace
and mercy. I will tell everyone I know about
what you have done for me. My life now has a
soundtrack, a song of thanksgiving.

For Forgiveness

The people around me are irritating me, God. With an apology on my lips, help me climb out of this rut of irritation and make amends. Help me learn from my mistakes and do better. Amen.

For Healing and Overcoming Illness

He healeth the broken in heart,
and bindeth up their wounds.

—Psalm 147:3

For Healing and Overcoming Illness

*And ye shall serve the Lord your God, and he shall bless thy
bread, and thy water; and I will take sickness away
from the midst of thee.*

—Exodus 23:25

We don't really know why we have to get sick,
Lord. We only know your promise: No matter where
we are or what we are called to endure, there you are
in the midst of it with us, never leaving our side. Not
for a split second. Thank you, Lord of all.

For Healing and Overcoming Illness

Heal me, O Lord, and I shall be healed; save me,
and I shall be saved: for thou art my praise.

—Jeremiah 17:14

Dear God,

The news of my illness terrified me, and I am feeling lost and afraid. I come to you asking for your healing and comfort as I go forward in dealing with my diagnosis. Without your support and love, my God, I am sure I won't be able to withstand the treatments and anxiety and fear, not just for myself, but for my family. In your arms I seek care and mercy. I seek the strength I need to return to good health. In your presence I know I will find my way and move towards a renewal of body, mind, and spirit. Help me, oh God, to stand against this challenge and win. Amen.

For Healing and Overcoming Illness

May the Lord keep you in his hand and never close his fist too tight on you.

For Healing and Overcoming Illness

Wherefore I say unto you, All manner of sin and blasphemy shall be forgiven unto men: but the blasphemy against the Holy Ghost shall not be forgiven unto men.

—Matthew 12:31

Holy Spirit, the life that gives life.

You are the cause of all movement;

You are the breath of all creatures;

You are the salve that purifies our souls;

You are the ointment that heals our wounds;

You are the fire that warms our hearts;

You are the light that guides our feet.

Let all the world praise you.

—Hildegard of Bingen

For Healing and Overcoming Illness

And hope maketh not ashamed; because the love of God is shed abroad in our hearts by the Holy Ghost which is given unto us.

—Romans 5:5

This illness has been my companion for a long time, Lord Jesus. I've prayed countless times for it to leave, but it remains nevertheless. I've been told just as many times that no answer to my pleas is still an answer from you and that you're not ignoring me. But, Lord, I still wonder why you won't heal me. I read about your compassion for the sick in the gospels, and they give me both hope and disappointment—hope because you can heal and disappointment because I haven't been healed. Please, Lord, increase my faith in you—not so much for you to heal me but to remind me that you are doing what is best for me. I pray that this illness will draw me even closer to you.

For Healing and Overcoming Illness

◆

In thankfulness for present mercy, nothing so becomes us as losing sight of past ills.

—Lew Wallace

For Healing and Overcoming Illness

I sought the Lord, and he heard me,
and delivered me from all my fears.

—Psalm 34:4

Deliver me, O God, from a slothful mind, from all lukewarmness, and all dejection of spirit. I know these cannot but deaden my love to you; mercifully free my heart from them, and give me a lively, zealous, active, and cheerful spirit, that I may vigorously perform whatever you command, thankfully suffer whatever you choose for me, and be ever ardent to obey in all things your holy love.

—John Wesley

For Healing and Overcoming Illness

And in that same hour he cured many of their infirmities and plagues, and of evil spirits; and unto many that were blind he gave sight.

—Luke 7:21

Dear God, you have sustained me through my illness. You have nursed my injury. You are my true physician, and I glorify you with all my heart. Amen.

For Healing and Overcoming Illness

Is any sick among you? let him call for the elders of the a church; and let them pray over him, anointing him with oil in the name of the Lord . . .

—James 5:14

When illness strikes, the effects go beyond the physical suffering. Fear, despair, and terrible isolation arise as the illness prolongs itself. It feels natural to lash out at your failing body, medicine that does not help, and even at the God who allowed this terrible thing to happen to you. The fate of the patient's loved ones can be equally painful, as they stand by feeling helpless to be of any real assistance. Yet, be assured that the Lord is there among you.

For Healing and Overcoming Illness

*For I reckon that the sufferings of this
present time are not worthy to be compared with
the glory which shall be revealed in us.*

—Romans 8:18

Despite today's valley of shadow and sickness,
I know you, shepherd of my soul, will continue
restoring me as I move through treatment to the safe
meadow of wellness.

For Healing and Overcoming Illness

It shall be health to thy navel, and marrow to thy bones.

—Proverbs 3:8

Help me recover from this ambush of illness, Great Physician, and the worry it brings. Reassure my fearful heart that my sickness was never intended; it just happened. Bodies break down, parts age, and minds weary. Your assurance gives me strength to hang on.

For Healing and Overcoming Illness

Heal the sick, cleanse the lepers, raise the dead, cast out devils:
freely ye have received, freely give.

—Matthew 10:8

Thank you, Great Physician, for this chance—
this second chance at life. Forgive me for being
surprised, as if healing were beyond possibility and
your intention.

For Healing and Overcoming Illness

And the blind and the lame came to him in the temple;
and he healed them.

—Matthew 21:14

Thank God when the pain ends, when once again we're well and whole and strong. Thank God when our bodies are released from the blinding, mind-numbing hurts that affect our whole lives. Thank God when we have complete victory over pain.

For Healing and Overcoming Illness

Pleasant words are as an honeycomb, sweet to the soul,
and health to the bones.

—Proverbs 16:24

*L*ord, help them, comfort them, and bring them peace and sweet, pain-free sleep. Ease the tension in their bodies and the ache in their hearts. Heal their hurts, please, Lord, and let them rest easy.

For Healing and Overcoming Illness

Then shall thy light break forth as the morning, and thine health shall spring forth speedily: and thy righteousness shall go before thee; the glory of the Lord shall be thy reward.

—Isaiah 58:8

Dear Lord,

Someone I love is very sick and I am asking in prayer for a healing. I am afraid and anxious for this person and pray for a quick recovery to strength and wholeness again. I also seek guidance, Lord, in how I might best be able to help this person and be there for the support, comfort, and love they need most. I seek to be an angel and offer what I can and to not be an extra burden to someone already dealing with stress and worry. Please wrap this person in your arms of love, security and caring and be a beacon of light in a time of darkness so that they might not lose hope. Amen.

For Healing and Overcoming Illness

Taking a deep breath is good medicine,
providing you breathe in the breath of God.

For Healing and Overcoming Illness

God,

Why is there so much disease in the world? So many of my friends are dealing with cancer, heart disease, and other major illnesses. I come to you in prayer today to ask for healing for all those who battle against a mental or physical illness. May they find strength and courage in your presence, enough to continue having faith that they will be restored to wellness again. May they find in your everlasting love a soothing balm to ease their pain and suffering. May they find a reason to keep on fighting each day and a purpose to their illness that makes them stronger, wiser, and more understanding. May they find hope. Amen.

For Healing and Overcoming Illness

And make straight paths for your feet, lest that which is lame be turned out of the way; but let it rather be healed.

—Hebrews 12:13

This seeing the sick endears them to us, us too it endears.

My tongue had taught thee comfort, touch had quenched thy tears.

—Gerard Manley Hopkins

For Healing and Overcoming Illness

He giveth power to the faint; and to them that have no might he increaseth strength.

—Isaiah 40:29

*L*ord Jesus, you are medicine to me when I am sick, strength to me when I need help, life itself when I fear death, the way when I long for heaven, the light when all is dark, and food when I need nourishment. Glory be to you forever. Amen.

—St. Ambrose

For Healing and Overcoming Illness

*O Lord my God, I cried unto thee, and thou hast healed me. O
Lord, thou hast brought up my soul from the grave: thou hast
kept me alive, that I should not go down to the pit.*

—Psalm 30:2–3

Dear God,

I come to you today humbled and grateful for the powerful
healing you have given me. I was so ill and broken, and weak
in body and spirit, and I was losing my faith that I would
ever feel good again. Yet you took care of me. Your love
provided me with all the medicine I could ever need, and the
hope of your eternal presence motivated me to stay in faith,
even when things seemed so bleak. I thank you from the
bottom of my heart for this new sense of well-being and
health, and for knowing that if I stay positive and hopeful,
your loving will for me will prevail over any disease or
challenge. Amen.

For Healing and Overcoming Illness

Cast thy burden upon the Lord, and he shall sustain thee: he shall never suffer the righteous to be moved.

—Psalm 55:22

Take this burden from me, Lord,
Free me from this pain.
Let me move with ease and grace
And walk in health again.
Take this yoke upon you, Lord,
And help me toward my goal,
I'm tired of being sick and tired
And long to be made whole.
Release me from my illness
And restore me to my best.
If you can do that for me, Lord,
I'll take care of the rest.

For Healing and Overcoming Illness

I have seen his ways, and will heal him: I will lead him also,
and restore comforts unto him and to his mourners.

—Isaiah 57:18

If your body suffers pain, and your health you can't
regain, and your soul is almost sinking in despair, Jesus
knows the pain you feel, he can save and he can heal,
take your burden to the Lord and leave it there.

—Charles Albert Tindley

For Healing and Overcoming Illness

Let my cry come near before thee, O Lord:
give me understanding according to thy word.

—Psalm 119:169

Creator God, you have come to me with healing in your hand. When I cried out, you heard me. You provided me with a gift that brought both peace and pleasure to my harried life. You helped me to focus on life instead of illness and sorrow. Lord, thank you for this wondrous gift. Amen.

For Healing and Overcoming Illness

Let my supplication come before thee:
deliver me according to thy word.

—Psalm 119:170

Heal us, Emmanuel, hear our prayer; we wait to feel thy touch; deep-wounded souls to thee repair, and Savior, we are such.

—William Cowper

For Healing and Overcoming Illness

There is no fear in love; but perfect love casteth out fear: because fear hath torment. He that feareth is not made perfect in love.

—1 John 4:18

Dear God, I am scared. I hear the doctor's approaching footsteps, but I do not know what news the doctor brings. Please help me to use my fear that it may become energy to live more fully, with more appreciation, from this day on. Amen.

For Healing and Overcoming Illness

To another faith by the same Spirit; to another the gifts of healing by the same Spirit . . .

—1 Corinthians 12:9

I cry out to you, O Lord, from the belly of my fear. In this dark pit of anxiety and confusion over my health, I ask that you reach in and guide me into the light of day. My faith in you is strong, and my trust in you is steadfast. Come to my aid, O Lord, as you did when Jonah called to you. Amen

For Healing and Overcoming Illness

How can I myself alone bear your cumbrance, and your burden, and your strife?

—Deuteronomy 1:12

Mental illness can be so devastating, Lord. Few understand the heartaches involved in diseases that carry no apparent physical scars. Be with those friends, neighbors, and family members who deal daily with difficult situations of which we are often unaware. Touch them with your special love, and let them know that they can lean on you, Lord. Ease their burdens, quell their sadness, and calm their desperation. Bring peace and healing to these households.

For Healing and Overcoming Illness

*Behold, I will bring it health and cure, and I will cure them,
and will reveal unto them the abundance of peace and truth.*

—Jeremiah 33:6

Pray always, while you eat and sleep.
Pray in your dreams, that the prophets may appear
And give you true vision.
Pray that your road in life
Will follow the footsteps of the Lord,
That you may not mistake death for life nor sorrow for joy,
That your soul, now a half-dead sparrow with broken wing,
Shall be fed, and cured, until at the peak of health
He begins his journey, the flight towards the sun.

—Author Unknown

For Healing and Overcoming Illness

Watch, dear Lord, with those who wake, or watch, or weep
tonight, and give your angels charge over those who sleep.
Tend your sick ones, O Lord Christ,
Rest your weary ones.
Bless your dying ones.
Soothe your suffering ones.
Pity your afflicted ones.
Shield your joyous ones.
And all for your love's sake. Amen.

—St. Augustine

For Healing and Overcoming Illness

There is a balm in Gilead
To make the wounded whole;
There is a balm in Gilead
To heal the sin-sick soul.
Some times I feel discouraged,
And think my work's in vain,
But then the Holy Spirit
Revives my soul again.
If you can't preach like Peter,
If you can't pray like Paul,
Just tell the love of Jesus,
And say He died for all.
There is a balm in Gilead
To make the wounded whole;
There is a balm in Gilead
To heal the sin-sick soul.

—African-American Spiritual

For Healing and Overcoming Illness

And who is he that will harm you,
if ye be followers of that which is good?

—1 Peter 3:13

Bless those who tend us when we are ailing in body, mind, and soul. They are a gift from you, Great Healer, sent to accompany us along the scary roads of illness. Bless their skills, potions, and bedside manners. Sustain them as they sustain us, for they are a channel of your love.

For Healing and Overcoming Illness

$\mathcal{A}$nd the prayer of faith shall save the sick, and the Lord shall raise him up; and if he have committed sins, they shall be forgiven him.

—James 5:15

For Healing and Overcoming Illness

Lord, how I hate being sick! It's hard to function when I'm this way. Not only do I feel lousy, but I also don't want to spread my illness to others. And so, I feel both unwell and isolated, I suppose being sick and alone is a perfect time for me to commune with you—to share what I'm thinking and feeling and listen to what you want me to and do with my life. Thank you, Lord, for grabbing my attention in this way. Otherwise, I might be too busy to hear what you have to say to me. Please keep me grounded in you. I pray in Jesus' precious name. Amen.

For Healing and Overcoming Illness

*Verily, verily, I say unto you, That ye shall weep and lament,
but the world shall rejoice: and ye shall be sorrowful,
but your sorrow shall be turned into joy.*

—John 16:20

Lord, I am now in tribulation, and my heart is ill at ease, for I am much troubled with the present suffering. . . . Grant me patience, O Lord, even now in this moment. Help me, my God, and then I will not fear, how grievously so ever I be afflicted.

—Thomas à Kempis